SHORT STORIES OF THE OLD WEST

WALTER A. ABBOTT

Short Stories Of The Old West
Copyright © 2022 by Walter A. Abbott

All rights reserved. No part of this publication may be reproduced, distributed, or transmitted in any form or by any means, including photocopying, recording, or other electronic or mechanical methods, without the prior written permission of the author, except in the case of brief quotations embodied in critical reviews and certain other non-commercial uses permitted by copyright law.

ISBN
978-1-956161-99-1 (Paperback)
978-1-956161-98-4 (eBook)

TABLE OF CONTENTS

WAY OF THE COMANCHE 1
BLEU SABOTEURS 6
BLUE RAVEN 15
CHOGAN 22
DEVIL'S RANGE 33
ENSENADA 42
FORSAKEN 51
HELL'S GATE 60
I AM MY BROTHER'S KEEPER 67
INCIDENT ON THE SNAKE RIVER 83
JESSIE SUTTER 94
MADELINE MCQUINN 102
MISSEY BLUE 112
RIVER OF REDEMPTION 120
THE DEVIL'S RIM 125
THE STRANGER 136
WINTER OF DESPERATION 148
WINTER'S BLOOD 155
TOO SAD TO CRY 161
ALTERNATIVE ENDING TO: TOO SAD TO CRY 171
SHADOWS OF DARKNESS 177

WAY OF THE COMANCHE

The year was 1842 in the New Mexico territory. The night was cold and windy with rain blowing in from the North. The stars disappeared behind the dark clouds. The last thing I remember was being in the barn attending to the new colt that had been born a week before. I was sitting with the colt's head in my lap under a lantern hanging overhead.

My father had just yelled out, "It's time to come in for the night son; you can see the colt tomorrow."

"Okay, I will be right there," I shouted back as I turned the lantern down and blew out the tiny flame before leaving the barn. The rain was falling harder and I could barely make out light in the cabin across from the barn. I had just closed the barn doors when I heard the sound of horses and yelling through the falling rain, coming over the hill towards the house. I ran to the front porch and then inside the cabin closing the door behind me placing a bar across the entrance. My father grabbed his rifle and mother was screaming, huddled in the corner of the bedroom in the rear of the cabin. The cabin was surrounded by Indians yelling and screaming. Before any one could move three Indians broke down the bar holding the door in place. They were Comanche, feared by everyone in the small valley. My father shot and killed one of the braves before one of the warriors drew his tomahawk and slashed open my father's head, killing him instantly. Another brave grabbed my mother by the hair, with a determined look while he drew his knife across her throat, before dropping her to the floor.

I was terrified and had nowhere to run. I started for the front door but was stopped by another brave who picked me up off my feet and carried me outside. Several others lit torches and threw them inside the cabin and the barn.

The horse and the young colt in the barn started to scream in a high shrilling tone; they were caught up in the fire with nowhere to escape. One of the braves grabbed me from behind then threw me up over his horse then jumped on behind me before riding off with the others in the dark of the night. I remember looking back to see the cabin and the barn burning. I was so scared I didn't know what to think or do. Both of my parents had been killed, in what seemed like moment of rage, and I was taken captive for a reason too young to understand. We rode all night and into the next morning before the Comanche village came in view. As we came upon the encampment the teepees lined a small stream running several hundred feet through a valley. The warriors were greeted by shouting women, young children and other braves. It was though they were being honored for whatever they had done while away. There were no spoils just a young terrified boy brought back to the village. The last I remember was that I was taken inside one of the lodges and left standing in front of a buffalo robe. Though I couldn't understand what was being said, a brave pointed towards the robe motioning for me to lie down. I knew what I was expected to do and try to go to sleep. I slept, in-between sobbing the entire night. I had no idea why I had not been killed along with my father and mother, eventually I would be given the answer.

The following morning the brave who had taken me inside his teepee nudged me to get up and come with him. I was taken to a small grove of trees where the other children playing began throwing rocks and sticks at me along the way; I was an unwelcome white intruder. The brave holding me by the hand yelled something at the children driving them away. I was given to a pretty Indian woman who took me by the hand and tried to comfort me by leading me to an area where she had been cooking something. She had something in a kettle that looked like porridge and gave me a spoon and motioned for me to eat. I had not eaten for over a day and was starving. Though I was reluctant to try the porridge I took a bite and found it to be quite good. I devoured the entire kettle. The woman laughed as I rubbed my stomach showing satisfaction for her food. I smiled and looked into her eyes. She was gentile and I didn1 t fear her as I had the others.

Over the next few days she tried to teach me her name which was Amisha, (meaning beauty) along with Comanche sign language so that I could communicate at some level. Amisha told me her husband1 s name was, Wahid (meaning unique). The weeks and months that followed I grew beyond my fear, realizing I would not be killed. I was treated like any other child in the camp and was directed to start learning from the other children. I had never been around other children, especially young Comanchel s. They seemed to laugh and enjoy life much like white children did, which surprised me. During moments of thought I would wander around the encampment walking by the river. I did this on a regular basis and was given the name Noconah, a Comanche word {meaning one who wanders). I joined the other children and learned how to play hoops which was a favorite past time. They were slowly beginning to accept me as one of them, though I still didn't understand much of what they were saying. The woman who cared for me and her husband were good to me and treated me well.

The woman made leggings and a small vest for me from soft deer skin. My hair had grown long and hung in a braid down my back. My skin had turned brown in the sun resembling the other children. I began to understand why the pretty Indian woman and her husband were caring for me. Following several years the truth came out, they had lost their only son to small pox years before. I was given to Amisha and Wahid to replace their dead son.

After my family and moved into the valley the Comanche's watched me grow until I was old enough to be taken into the tribe to be raised as a Comanche. I was told that had the Comanche treated my mother and father as intruders they would have been tortured first. The Comanche were there to take me and raise me as one of their own. That' s why my parents were not left to suffer but to die quickly.

My adopted father and mother did their best to raise me as one of their own and to teach me the Comanche ways of life. I began to realize that the Comanche were not wild and vicious killers. Their love for their own people created the reason to kill my parents and raise me as their own. It was not for their hatred of my father and mother, rather concerned about the loss of another little boy.

Months passed and I became taller and much stronger. I was made a special bow and given a set of arrows made by the Tribe's arrow maker. I became proficient with bow and arrows. I learned how to hunt and make a kill with one shot. After killing deer and larger game I joined the hunt for buffalo along with the best hunters in the tribe. When warriors left on raiding parties I was not asked to go with them and fight against my own people, only other tribes. Though the Comanche had a reputation for raiding and killing it was out of need not hatred or desire to kill someone, only to provide for their own people.

When I was about sixteen years old I began to look at other young women in the tribe of my own age. One of the women stood out above all others. She was pretty as my adopted mother; in fact she reminded me of her at a much younger age. There was something about her that attracted her to me. It may have been her shyness or her luring way of teasing. Either way I had grown fond of her. One day I asked a friend what her name was. She told me her name was Zitkala (meaning bird). From that moment on I called her by name which surprised her at first after which she realized how I found out. I had no idea that she was the daughter of the Arrow maker whose name was Hoekwai (meaning he who hunts). Zitkala and I would spend time each day walking along the river or riding our ponies across the countryside . Two years had passed and I knew I wanted to spend the rest of my life with her and raise a family together in the Comanche way. By now I had forgotten most of the English I once knew. It had slowly been replaced with Comanche. I grew to understand how much I loved Amisha and Wahid, my Comanche parents and how difficult it had been for them as well as me to become integrated into their family and be treated as their son. My future would be much different now, especially having fallen in love with Zitkala. I decided to discuss the matter with Hoekwai. He was always more than gracious to me and invited me to sit down and smoke for a while and discuss his daughter and me.

Hoekwai started the conversation by saying," I have watched you grow form the moment you came into the tribe as a young scared white boy. I was surprised that you were able to make the transition as well as you did. You have grown and embraced the Comanche way of life. I don't consider you to be a Whiteman any longer. You are a good man and your white parents would be proud of you if they were still alive. It is obvious you have a deep like for my daughter Zitkala." Hoekwai hesitated before saying," What is it that you want to say?"

"I have come to know you well over the years long before I met and fell in love with your daughter. I am here today to ask her hand in marriage but not without your blessing. I am concerned about one thing though, I am white and she is not! In your eyes does this mean we should not marry?"

"You are no longer white in the eyes of my people. You have shed your white past and have become Comanche. I would welcome you as my son-in- law and your offspring. I would consider it an honor!"

The following day I asked Zitkala for her hand in marriage and she readily accepted. The chief and the medicine man consecrated our marriage and we were taken to a separate teepee away from all the others. This is where we were to spend the next several days together away from he others to become more intimate and private.

The old ways were gone and my life would be changed forever as I

walked through life in the footsteps of a Comanche raising a family and finding what was the most important thing in life; it was not the color of a person's skin but the love in our heart that binds each of us to one-another along with everlasting knowledge of being loved by our family.

"I closed my tablet which concluded my interview and the story of Noconah, the white boy who became a Comanche. Noconah passed away shortly after this interview in 1921at the age of 83.

BLEU SABOTEURS

"My husband, it is time. The baby is ready to be born," Wahnayawah said.

"Let me prepare everything, then I will bring the pony for you. Then we shall go into the woods," Running Wolf replied. It had snowed the night before, and the ground was cold and crusty with snow. Running Wolf packed extra blankets and linens for the birth of the baby. He brought a pony for Wahnayawah and himself. Running Wolf climbed down from his pony and went inside their lodge; he brought Wahnayawah outside and helped her get on the pony.

The bearing-down pains were more frequent, and Wahnayawah knew there was little time left. Running Wolf led Wahnayawah through the snow deep into the woods where she could have the baby in private. Running Wolf would stay nearby and make sure there was no one else or any animals in the area. Wahnayawah slowly climbed down from her pony and walked over the crunchy snow to a small grove of trees where she could squat down between two small trees to support her. She lay out the blanket on the snowy ground with the muslin on top. Wahnayawah was having serious contractions and was breathing faster while pushing down at the same time. Finally the baby began to drop, falling on the muslin beneath her. With the umbilical cord still attached, the baby started to cry.

Wahnayawah reached down to pick up her baby when someone placed their hand over her mouth. Before she could jerk away, another person drew a knife across her throat, slitting it before dropping her to the ground. Wahnayawah was trying to hold her throat, but she kept gasping for air as the blood gurgled out of her mouth and stained the white snow. With her final gasp, she fell over dead facedown into the powdery snow.

Running Wolf was becoming concerned for his wife and decided to ride slowly to where her pony was to make sure she was all right. He then climbed down from his pony and started to walk toward the grove of trees. As he came closer, he saw a trail of blood and then Wahnayawah's body lying in the snow. Running Wolf ran to her then rolled her over. He picked her up. Running Wolf could see her throat had been slashed. He drew up her limp blood-soaked body clad in a buckskin dress and caressed her. He cried out and began to sing a death chant as he held her in his arms. She was dead and the baby gone. Running Wolf kneeled in the wet snow, while holding Wahnayawah and rocking her in his arms. His face was pale, and his heart was filled with grief. Every worldly pleasure and love had been stripped from his soul.

After regaining his composure, Running Wolf tied Wahnayawah's petite body over her pony then led her pony back to the village. When Running Wolf arrived, everyone surrounded him; they wanted to see the new baby. Running Wolf walked over to Wahnayawah's pony, cut her loose, and then eased her savagely violated body to the ground. There was silence; no one knew nor could they understand what had happened out there. Slain Deer, a close friend of Running Wolf's, asked what happened. Running Wolf could hardly speak; he was in shock, and the reality of what happened had not set in.

Slain Deer put his arms around Running Wolf in an effort to comfort him, but Running Wolf turned away and headed back to his lodge. Without any explanation, Running Wolf asked everyone to leave him alone, that he needed to give this matter some serious thought in private. Later that day, Running Wolf came out of his lodge and told everyone how he found Wahnayawah without the baby.

Running Wolf said to everyone, "I blame myself. I was there to make sure nothing happened to either Wahnayawah or the baby, and now they are both gone because of me. I will find the killer of my wife and what became of our baby. I will rest no more or find peace within my soul until vengeance is mine."

The following morning, Running Wolf rode back to where Wahnayawah's body was found. He scoured the area, looking for any sign of either white men or Indians who might have killed Wahnayawah and taken the baby. Running Wolf walked in a circle around Wahnayawah's body, making a larger and larger circle, looking for any sign. About fifty yards through a clearing, he came across horseshoe prints of two horses and riders. The tracks were below the hill and the grove of trees where

Wahnayawah's body was found. These could have been the two riders who killed his wife and took the baby. Running Wolf bent down to take a closer look at the horseshoe prints in the ground. These were not Indian ponies; both were shod. The shoes had strange markings resembling an *S* stamped in each one. They were either white men or someone else. Running Wolf had never seen these markings before. After carefully searching the area all day, Running Wolf found no other signs of anyone else having been there.

The nearest settlement was a trading post twenty miles to the south. He and his people had been at peace with the white settlers. Running Wolf decided to ride to the settlement to find out more about the strange markings on the shoeprints. He and the fort's commander, Captain Ellis Hatcher, had been longtime friends.

"Running Wolf, what brings you to the fort?" Captain Hatcher asked.

"It is a serious matter," Running Wolf explained. After telling the captain about the death of his wife and his stolen baby, he asked the captain if he knew of anyone else having problems with killings by people with strange markings on the shoes of their horses.

"I am terribly sorry to hear of your wife's death and the disappearance of your baby. You know, come to think of it, I did receive a telegram a couple of weeks ago about some problems north of here and into Canada. The information was about a French militia calling themselves the Bleu Saboteurs. They were out of Quebec and were seeking retribution towards the whites over the Louisiana Purchase. They claimed that President Jefferson took advantage of the French government in the process of acquiring that area for the United States. Running Wolf, I don't know if this has anything to do with your wife's death and your baby, but it could be a possibility, though you are an Indian."

"Thank you, Captain. I will look for these men and find out if they are the killers and if they have my baby."

"Be careful. These men are professional soldiers and killers. Don't try to deal with them on your own," the captain warned.

Running Wolf jumped on his horse and galloped off heading north. If it took Running Wolf the rest of his life, he would find these men and determine if they were the killers and whether they took his baby; then he would deal with them in his own way. His heart had become hardened, and no mercy would be spared; his life was changed forever. Running Wolf changed his identity by dressing and acting like a poor Indian.

As he rode north, the weather became worse with frequent snowstorms and blinding winds. Two weeks of hard riding brought Running Wolf to a small village where everyone spoke broken English. He tried to inquire about the French militia, but no one would discuss it with him. They were afraid to discuss it. Something strange was going on, and Running Wolf would find out what it was. That night, Running Wolf waited outside a saloon for one of the girls to come outside. A short petite blonde walked out of the saloon just after it closed for the night. Running Wolf followed her to a small shack at the end of the street. The woman stepped up to unlock the door when Running Wolf came up behind her; he placed his hand over her mouth and told her not to scream; he just wanted to ask her something. She nodded okay, and he released his grip over her face.

"Have you heard of the Bleu Saboteurs?" The woman's face turned white with fear, and she began to cry.

"My name is Running Wolf. I am not here to scare you. I just need some answers."

Running Wolf tried to comfort the woman. He then asked her what she knew about the soldiers and told her what happened to his wife and his baby.

"They are nothing but killers seeking revenge for something no one here knows about," the woman said.

"What is your name?"

"My name is Amarante Floteur," she replied.

"I am Running Wolf, and I am dressed this way to find the answers I need. I plan to kill every one of those men after I find them. What have they done to you or the people that live here?"

"Twenty-seven men and several pack mules came riding into our village about five days ago, killing three women and taking their babies with them. They told everyone if they said anything about what happened here, they would come back and kill everyone else. An old man asked one of the soldiers why they were here, and without saying a word, the soldier sitting on his horse turned and shot the old man in the head while everyone was watching. I was standing behind the old man, and his blood splattered over me and some of the others."

"Who took the babies?" Running Wolf asked.

"They were given to two women in a wagon that appeared to be filled with ammunition. They took the babies then hurried to the wagon before leaving."

"Did you see which way the soldiers went when they rode out of town?"

"They rode south towards a small town of Good Hope. It is about fifty miles from here," Amarante replied.

"I will tell no one of our conversation, but I want you to be careful. When I am finished, I will return," Running Wolf said.

Running Wolf bought provisions from the local mercantile then left for Good Hope. Running Wolf slept by day and traveled at night, avoiding possible sentries or soldiers. The fourth day it began to snow hard. Running Wolf decided to take a chance and ride on through the storm toward Good Hope. As night approached, Running Wolf arrived at the outskirts of town. He tied up his pony and decided to walk in under the cover of night and explore the situation. Running Wolf searched for the ammunition wagon and the two women. He found the wagon behind a building on Main Street.

There was a French guard in front of the wagon walking back and forth. Running Wolf worked his way behind the wagon and crawled underneath it until he was at the front. As the guard approached, he grabbed him by both legs, dragging him to the ground, then slit his throat. He pushed the body under the wagon. He then climbed upon the wagon and quietly pulled back the flap where he could see inside the wagon.

The two women inside were holding the babies and caring for them. When they looked up, they saw Running Wolf motioning for them to be quiet. They didn't say a word; they were more scared than anything else. Running Wolf told them who he was, and a sigh of relief came over their faces.

"I want to know which baby is mine," he asked. One of the women held up a baby boy who was his son. Running Wolf extended his arms, and his son was placed in them. He wept and was thankful that the women had taken good care of him along with the other two babies. Initially the women were frightened; they thought they might be taken away and killed by the soldiers. The women told Running Wolf that they were captives from another village and that their lives were in danger. Running Wolf told them to act normal; they must trust him, and everything would be all right.

Running Wolf knew that other soldiers would find the dead man's body and would start looking for him. Late that night, two soldiers came by the wagon looking for the guard. The women inside were questioned, but they told the men they had heard nothing. The two men left, and the next day the village was turned upside down looking for the dead guard. The villagers were threatened and told if they were hiding information they would be shot. No one knew anything about what had happened. The guard had disappeared.

Two days later another woman and her baby were taken hostage and placed in the wagon with the other two women. The French militia was ready to leave. The team was hooked up to the wagon, and everyone began to leave. Someone noticed the dead guard lying on the ground after the wagon had pulled forward.

"Over here!" one of the men yelled. "It looks like a body."

The *capitaine* rode over to the wagon and climbed down from his black stallion.

He walked over to the body then rolled it over. "It is Per'sant. His throat has been cut." The capitaine stopped the caravan and had his men bring everyone into the street. The capitaine said, "If we have to, we will kill everyone here unless we find the killer first." He motioned for one of his men to interrogate each person one at a time, demanding they say who killed the French guard. No one knew; they hadn't seen the French guard killed.

The capitaine directed his officers to pull every third person out of the line and start executing them one at time until the truth was heard. The first man was run through with a sword. The second was a woman whose throat was slit. The third was a young boy who was shot in the head. The others begged for their lives.

"Well, I guess no one knows who did the killing!" The capitaine laughed. The caravan left the village, moving further south. Running Wolf had scouted out the area ahead of the militia and waited for them in a mountainous area. Two days later the French militia entered a narrow opening that led into a narrow mountain pass before crossing into an open area five miles away.

After the capitaine had led his men into the narrow part of the pass, Running Wolf was ready to set off the dynamite planted in the rocks on one side of the narrows before crossing into the open area. Running Wolf sat on the side of the rocky mountain, patiently waiting for the caravan to enter the pass. When the militia reached the narrow part of the pass, he set off the dynamite. Running Wolf made sure he did not hit the wagon with the women and babies trailing behind. The side of the mountain gave way; the rocks rained down on the caravan, killing fifteen of the soldiers. Screams could be heard echoing down the canyon as soldiers were buried under a mountain of rocks and debris.

The capitaine signaled for the others to turn around and go back through the pass as fast as possible and seek cover. While the capitaine was leading his men out of the pass, Running Wolf shot two soldiers with arrows from his mountain side perch. Eighteen men had been killed, leaving only nine, including the capitaine. Fear was running through the minds of those who were still alive, not knowing who might be next to die. The remaining men and wagon were running for their lives out of the pass, trying to reach an open area.

Running Wolf scaled down the mountain as quickly as he could. He jumped on his horse at the bottom and followed after the remaining French soldiers. He stayed far behind them. That night Running Wolf knew they would have to stop and make camp. He planned his final attack, planning to kill the rest.

After darkness fell Running Wolf made his way into the outskirts of the camp. There were three guards surrounding the campsite. The first guard was attending the horses. Running Wolf crept slowly through the brush until he was directly behind the guard. He did not want to take any chances; he reached around the man's head and jerked it back while he thrust the knife into the man's chest. Running Wolf dropped the man to the ground then dragged him into some undergrowth.

About fifty yards away Running Wolf spotted another guard. He moved slowly toward the man.

When he was in full view Running Wolf drew back his bow and shot the man with an arrow. The arrow struck the man in the heart, killing him instantly.

Running Wolf moved his body behind a large piece of fallen timber. The last guard was standing about forty yards away. Running Wolf whispered something to lure the man to him. The guard slowly walked toward Running Wolf with his gun cocked and ready to shoot.

The man was about ten feet away when Running Wolf said, "Over here!"

The man turned toward Running Wolf at the same time Running Wolf brandished his tomahawk and hurled it at the man, striking him in the head. The man let out a cry before falling to the ground. The other militia members were inside a large tent eating around a makeshift table. Running Wolf took an arrow and wrapped dried bark around the obsidian tip, striking it on the ground to ignite the bark. He shot the burning arrow into the tent, setting it on fire. Suddenly men started to run out of the tent in different directions. Running Wolf shot five of the men with arrows and knifed one of them as he came nearby; after leaving the burning tent, only the capitaine remained and was the last man out. He came out firing into the night; he was terrified of whoever was out there. His life was now on the line.

The capitaine screamed, "Come out, coward, so I can see you!"

Running Wolf stepped out of the shadows, looking the capitaine directly in the eyes.

"Who are you?" the capitaine demanded.

"The only thing you need to know is I am here to see that you are punished for the terrible things you and your men have done to me and the others."

The capitaine lunged at Running Wolf with a sword in hand. Running Wolf stepped aside and hit the capitaine in the face, knocking him to the ground. Running Wolf jumped on top of the capitaine then brought him to his feet and tied his hands behind his back with rawhide.

"What are you going to do with me?" the capitaine yelled.

"I am not going to do anything. That will be up to the villagers at Good Hope." Running Wolf tied a rope around the capitaine's neck and told him to walk ahead of the wagon.

"You will keep walking until I tell you to stop. Do you understand?" Running Wolf asked.

"Yes, sir," the capitaine replied.

Two days later the wagon along with the capitaine arrived at Good Hope. The capitaine was near death, and he collapsed on the street.

The villagers came running out to see what was happening.

Everyone saw Running Wolf on the wagon seat with the three women and babies in the back. Everyone shouted for joy.

Someone said, "What are we to do with this man?"

"You can do whatever you want with him. He is your prisoner. The other twenty-six are dead. He is the last of the Bleu Saboteurs."

Several men ran out and dragged the capitaine off the street to the jailhouse. Amarante made her way to Running Wolf through the crowd.

"I am glad you are still alive. I knew somehow you would come back," Amarante said.

The next day Running Wolf took his baby boy and left the village with Amarante. The townspeople had a short trial; they decided to burn the capitaine at the stake in the town square so that no one would ever forget what happened there.

BLUE RAVEN

The morning was warm with a gentle breeze from the south rustling the corn tassels. Blue Raven and her friends were Santee; they had been weeding the village field of corn, which was located about a hundred yards from the main encampment situated along the banks of the Missouri River. Blue Raven and other girls had been working since early morning. Blue Raven looked across several rows and saw something lying in one of the trenches between the corn stocks. She cautiously approached, what looked like a man just lying face down. Blue Raven bent over to see if the man was dead or alive. Suddenly the man turned to one side and grabbed her pulling her to the ground. He drew his knife and placed it across her throat.

"If you shout, I will slit your throat. Do you understand?" Blue Raven could only nod under the firm grasp of the man. The man proceeded to take his knife and cut away Blue Raven's skin dress while holding his hand over her mouth. When he was done he left Blue Raven lying on the ground with her dress slit and blood running down her legs.

"If you tell anyone about what happened, I will return and burn your village to the ground!" The man slowly moved away from the corn patch on his hands and knees, making his way back into a stand of trees. He mounted his horse and rode off with another man waiting for him. Blue Raven had been violated and would never be allowed to marry in the tribe as she was now a soiled woman, unsuitable for marriage. She violated the sacred rights of her tribe and would never be accepted in the village again. She lay on the ground sobbing and hurting. Her heart was filled with shame as she had become a victim of the white man.

The sun was up and the other women had returned to the village to find shade in the heat of the day. Blue Raven was sickened and attempted to crawl away from the field where she could hide from the outside world. By the end of the day she had struggled to walk about three miles and sought shelter in a grove of trees at the base of a large rock. She knew that there would be a search party sent out to find her, but she could never be found and humiliated by her friends and the members of the tribe.

The next morning at dawn, she walked west until she came to a small stream. Blue Raven decided to walk in the stream as long as she could. This would help her from being followed by her people. She walked about two miles in the stream then decided to leave the stream and continued north. As the sun set, she was exhausted and weak because she had lost so much blood. She knew she couldn't continue much longer; she was growing weaker and weaker. On the horizon, Blue Raven could make out what looked like a wagon or stagecoach trail. She continued to walk toward it, but the sun was bearing down on her, taking her strength away.

She could walk no further and collapsed along the roadway, falling into the sagebrush.

Several hours later, she could hear the sound of horses and rolling wheels on the ground. She was too weak to even look up.

"Look over there, do you see someone?" the stage driver yelled out.

"Yaw, Herb, it looks like a body lying on the prairie!"

"Whoa," Herb said as he pulled back on the reins, "we better check it out." The stage rolled to a stop. Josh, the man riding shotgun, jumped down and walked over to the body. He bent over and saw a young Indian woman who was passed out and had dried blood on her dress and legs.

"Come over here, Herb, and bring the canteen. You need to see this!" Josh shouted. Herb jumped down from the stage and ran over to where Josh was.

"It looks like a young Santee girl. I can tell by the design work on her leggings. I wonder where she came from. Her moccasins are worn out. She must have walked a long way. The closest village has to be fifteen or twenty miles from here."

Josh bent over to listen for a heartbeat. "Well, she is alive, but she is in bad shape. Hand me the water and help me prop her up." Josh cradled her in his arms while Herb tried to give her water. She choked on the first swallow.

"Don't drown her, go easy. We need to get her to a doctor," Josh said.

"Why are we stopping out here in the middle of nowhere?" shouted one of the passengers.

"Just climb back inside. We have an Indian girl that has been hurt, and she needs attention. We will be on our way shortly!" Herb yelled. "We need a couple of men to help lift her on the stage."

"She's not riding inside with us. We don't want a stinking Indian riding along!" another man yelled.

"Shut up and get over here, she's not riding inside but on top. Are you going to help or just complain?" Herb asked. Two of the passenger helped carry Blue Raven to the stage.

Josh got on top and rolled out two blankets to lay her on.

"Okay, hand her up here but be careful!" Josh was able to secure Blue Raven and lay her down on top. He laid a blanket over her, partially covering her face to keep the hot sun from scorching her beautiful face.

"I will ride on top with her until we get back to town. I don't want her rolling off, and I don't want to tie her down. It could hurt her," Josh volunteered. Two hours later the stage rolled into town. Josh stayed on top while the passengers got out. Herb came over to the side and asked for a couple of men just standing around to help. Three men reached up as Josh handed Blue Raven to the men on the ground. "Take her over to the Doc Barrett's office, and I will meet you there!" one of the men shouted.

"Someone get the sheriff and tell him to meet us at the Doc's office," Josh shouted.

"Why bother? If she dies it will be a good thing. After all, we don't need another smelly Indian living here."

"She's human just like you are. She has the right to live just like anyone else!" Herb shouted. The men carried Blue Raven to the doc's office and laid her on the examination table.

"Everyone get out of here, I need to examine my patient," the doc said. The sheriff came to the door and knocked.

"Who is it?" the doc asked.

"It's me, the sheriff," Jesse answered.

"Come on in but just for a minute. This girl is in bad shape. I need to examine her right away."

"Okay, Doc, let me know what you think after you have examined her."

"All right, just go on back to your office and leave me alone," the doc said. An hour later the doc had completed his examination of Blue Raven then sent for the sheriff.

"Well, sheriff, she has been brutally raped and partially strangled, leaving bruise marks around her neck. Across her throat was a shallow knife wound. She had hemorrhaged internally and had lost much blood. It would be a long time before she would regain her health. I don't know who did this, but whoever did this should be shot on sight. This woman needs some clothes to wear. Can you get her a dress or something?" the doc said in a concerned tone.

"Yes, I'll go across the street. Mildred should have something for her. By the way, did she say anything to you, Doc?"

"She tried to say something, but I could not understand her. We need someone who speaks Sioux."

"Who in town speaks Sioux?"

"The only one I know is Butch Milner. I believe he was married to a Sioux for several years," the doc replied.

"Is he still around these parts, or did he go to California?" the sheriff asked.

"The last I heard he was living out on the old Yellow Creek homestead north of town."

"I will go on out there and see if he is around. He may be able to help us find out what happened." That afternoon the sheriff along with Butch arrived back in town. Butch and the sheriff walked over to the doc's office where Blue Raven was still lying on the examination table.

"Let me talk to her?" Butch asked. Butch proceeded to ask Blue Raven several questions, but the only answer she gave him was her name and where she was from.

"What did she say? "The sheriff asked?

"She told me her name was Blue Raven and that she was Santee, and her village was on the shore of the Missouri River. Her mother died giving birth, and her father was a renegade who abandoned her after she was born. She said she couldn't tell me who did this to her because she was afraid he would attack her village and kill everyone there."

"Whoever did this to her put the fear of God in her. It will be difficult to find the man without some help," the sheriff replied.

"One thing for sure, she is going to need somewhere to stay until she gets better or until she can return to her village," the doc said.

The sheriff was making inquiries all over town, trying to find a temporary home for Blue Raven. No one wanted an Indian woman living with them. One afternoon, an older couple homesteading a small piece of ground west of town came in for supplies. Charlie and Ruth Gorman were in their sixties and had lost two sons to the war. They were kindhearted and open-minded. The sheriff had known them for several years and considered them to be good friends. The sheriff noticed Charlie's wagon pull up in front of the trading post and walked over to see how they were doing.

In the course of conversation, the sheriff mentioned Blue Raven and what had happened to her and that no one in town would take her in, not even on a temporary basis.

Ruth turned to Charlie and said, "What do you think? We could use some help around the place."

"You know, I think it would be a good idea. We could use some help, and it sounds like she needs a family."

"Let me take you over to the doc's office and introduce you to her," the sheriff said. Following the introductions, Blue Raven rode out of town with the Gormans. It seemed they were well suited for each other. Blue Raven helped inside and outside, doing everything from washing the clothes to feeding the livestock. Blue Raven had been living with the Gormans for more than two months when she suddenly became ill and began throwing up. Blue Raven couldn't keep anything down; everything she ate came back up.

Ruth said, "Something is wrong. We need to get her to the doctor."

Charlie hitched up the horses while Ruth and Blue Raven sat on the buckboard waiting for Charlie to take them into town. Charlie pulled up in front of the doc's office and took Blue Raven inside.

"What brings you to town? It's nice to see you again," the doc said.

"Blue Raven is ill, and we don't know what's wrong with her," Charlie said.

"Bring her over here and sit her down on the table. Let me take a look at her," the doc said.

"Go on out Charlie. When I've finished I'll let you know how she is."

After the doc had examined Blue Raven he determined she was pregnant and that she would have to take things a little easier until after the baby arrived. The doc walked Blue Raven out to the wagon and told Charlie and Ruth the news. They were surprised, never having given it a thought. They knew what happened to Blue Raven, and the possibility loomed in the back of Ruth's mind.

Time went by, and a healthy baby boy arrived. Blue Raven was happy, as were Ruth and Charlie. It was as if it was their grandson. They had become so attached to Blue Raven and the boy they decided to let them stay on as long as they cared to. The baby was christened *Eneypay* (a Sioux word meaning "brave").

In the years that followed, Blue Raven and Eneypay greatly enjoyed the relationship with Charlie and Ruth and loved them dearly. They, in turn, were both loved as much as a daughter and a grandson could be. Eneypay grew up and was taught the ways of the white man and how to speak English. Blue Raven learned to speak English as well, being taught by Ruth.

When Eneypay was old enough, Blue Raven sat him down and told him what happened to her and how she became pregnant by a white man with deep-set light blue eyes and a two-sided scar over his right eye.

She told him why she never returned to her village, that she would be an outcast and considered unclean. Eneypay was called a half-breed most of his life while attending traditional schools. He was bright and very proficient with a handgun. Charlie had taught him how to draw and shoot in case the need arose. Eneypay was close to Charlie, and he called him Gampa Charlie. He grew strong and became the ranch foreman for Charlie and Ruth. They loved Blue Raven and Eneypay like their own. It was as if they were godsent, after losing their two sons.

Eneypay had doubled the herd and had extended the crops beyond the original homestead. Blue Raven and Eneypay had finally been accepted by the townspeople after all the years. They were invited to social occasions with or without the Gormans. It was October, and the annual harvest ball and dance were coming up this Saturday night at the town hall. The whole town was invited. Ruth asked Blue Raven and Eneypay if they would like to go with them.

Blue Raven was not sure, but Eneypay was ready to go either way.

"Now, dear, it will be good for you to get out and meet some nice men. I know it has been difficult, but I believe you will enjoy yourself and maybe even be asked to dance," Ruth said. Blue Raven finally relented and agreed to go but just for an hour. Everyone climbed on the buckboard and headed for town. They arrived in front of the town hall at about six thirty that evening. Charlie jumped off to tie up the horses when an explosion was heard down the street. It was the bank; it was being robbed. Eneypay jumped from the wagon and ran toward the bank as fast as he could. On the way the sheriff caught up with him.

"I will help," Eneypay shouted as he ran toward the bank with his gun drawn and ready to shoot. The sheriff and Eneypay were about fifty yards from the bank when one of the holdup men ran outside and shot the sheriff. He fell to the street; he had been shot in the chest.

Eneypay returned the fire and shot the outlaw in the arm. He dropped a saddlebag full of money and tried to mount his horse tied up in front of the bank, but he could not hold on; he fell onto the street. The third man came through the front door of the bank trying to shoot his way out. Eneypay shot the man on the boardwalk. He fell over dead. Eneypay ran to the other outlaw who finally was able to climb on his horse. The man was about to run off when Eneypay jumped upon the back of the horse and pulled the man off to the ground. Eneypay drew his knife and threatened to slit his throat if he tried to move. At that moment Eneypay looked the man in the eyes as he straddled him. His eyes were light blue and deep set, and there was the scar his mother had told him about. This must be his father.

"Go ahead and kill me, breed. That's what you want, isn't it?" the man screamed He couldn't kill him; instead, Eneypay slowly got up then threw his knife as far away as he could.

Several men were now surrounding the outlaw and picked him up and carried him to the sheriff's office and locked him up. Eneypay was so shaken he ran back to his mother who was waiting with open arms. They never talked about that day again, but somehow, Eneypay knew his mother was aware of who the outlaw was.

CHOGAN

The teepees were strewn along the winding stream. The morning was chilly with a hint of fall in the air, with winter close behind. Today everything would be dismantled in preparation to move the village to a warmer climate before winter set in. The days were long and arduous in search of a new site for the encampment. The camp dogs were barking as the wind started up. Everyone was still asleep, but the sun began to show itself in the east to greet the morning. The rush of water and the intermittent barking were the only sounds of the day. Chogan (Black Bird) slept inside the buffalo clad teepee with his father and mother.

The sound of many riders in the distance could be heard, alarming the dogs and waking everyone in the encampment. Before anyone had a chance to dress or grab weapons the riders rode into the camp with a fury of vengeance. Some of the riders pulled down teepees while others trampled women and children, tearing them apart under razor sharp hooves, while others were shot at close range. The chief ran out of his teepee barehanded and attempted to pull one of the men off his horse. He was shot in the head, splattering blood everywhere.

Chogan's father grabbed his bow and quiver as he ran from his teepee. He yelled at the others to stay inside. Before he could draw his bow he was shot twice, dropping him to the ground. Chogan was so scared he slid beneath a buffalo robe. His mother ran after his father. While she bent over Chogan's father, one of the riders buried a tomahawk in her head, killing her instantly. What seemed like hours passed in just minutes, leaving everyone dead but Chogan. Chogan waited until he heard no more noise before he slid out from beneath his buffalo robe.

Chogan was ten years old and had never experienced anything like this before. With death all around he ran to his parents, where he found his mother dead lying on top of his father. He was so scared he couldn't cry; he kneeled down beside them in the dust. Chogan laid his head on his mother while clinging to her as best as a young boy of his age could. His mother had a bear claw necklace around her neck which she wore for good luck. Chogan reached over and gently untied the rawhide strands holding the necklace around his mother's neck. With both hands wrapped around it he drew the necklace to his chest. Chogan slowly rose to his feet not knowing what to do or where to go.

Distraught, he began wandering around aimlessly, looking for anyone who may be alive. The sun was up with heat reigning down on this lost Indian child. As he walked through the village, he noticed empty cartridges lying on the ground. He reached down to pick one of them up and blew on it trying to make it whistle. He also saw horseshoe prints scattered everywhere, telling him that another tribe had not attacked; it was *wasicu* or white men.

Chogan had been taught many things by his father, whom he looked up to, wanting to become a great warrior like him. His father told him if ever he became lost to follow a river down the mountain that will eventually take him to a village or town. Chogan began to walk along the river across a plateau down the valley. After walking tirelessly all day in the fiery heat, Chogan was near exhaustion with nightfall looming on the horizon. He decided to cover himself with pine boughs to ward off the cold night. The following day Chogan was awakened by the sound of a fox chasing a rabbit across the meadow. Chogan was hungry and needed to find food. His mother had told him about wild berries and how to find them. He came upon a thicket of wild blueberries where he stopped and gorged himself until he could hold no more. Chogan continued down the mountain following the river, taking time out to rest as he continued. Three days later Chogan reached the valley floor. In the distance he could see a small house and some out buildings. He stumbled closer to the ranch house before collapsing in a nearby field.

Inside the ranch house a man said to his son, "Go out and bring the two mares into the barn before it starts to rain."

The young boy walked toward the horses but suddenly came upon Chogan, who was lying face down on the ground. "Dad, come here! There's an Indian boy in the field!" the young boy yelled. His father ran to his son and Chogan. He bent over and picked Chogan up then carried him to the house.

Margaret, his wife, stood at the door and said, "Bring the boy inside, he looks like he is starving to death. Lay him over there," pointing to a wolf skin lying in the corner spread out on the floor. Chogan was carefully laid on the wolf hide. He showed no sign of life other than he was still breathing.

"Father, where do you think he came from?" the son asked.

"I don't know. It appears he has been out there walking for days. I'm not sure which tribe he is from or what happened to him."

"Henry, what are we going to do with him?" Margaret asked? "He just can't stay here."

"I don't know. Right now the important thing is to get him back to better health and then find out who he is," Henry replied.

Chogan lay on the floor for two days before he was strong enough to speak. His eyes were wide open, filled with fear. He didn't know where he was or who these strangers were. He tried to get up and run, but he was unable to as he still suffered from fatigue. Margaret tried to calm Chogan by offering him a cup of water and something to eat. Chogan turned his head away out of fear.

"I don't know what to do with this boy if he doesn't eat or drink," Margaret remarked.

"He'll eat and drink when he gets hungry and thirsty enough. Just give him time," Henry said.

"How are we going to talk to him?" Margaret asked? "We don't know what tribe he is from or what language he speaks."

"I'm going to ride over to Jack Condor's place and ask him if he knows anyone who may be able to talk to the boy. I'll be back for supper," Henry said.

Henry reached Jack's ranch; after a lengthy conversation, Jack told him he had a man working for him by the name of Jean Moreau, who had been an interpreter at Fort Laramie.

"Henry, I would like to meet the Indian boy myself. Jean and I will ride over to your place this evening," Jack said.

"I appreciate your help. Why don't you plan on supper? You know Margaret is a good cook!"

Later that evening Jean had a lengthy conversation with Chogan. He was able to determine which tribe and which part of the country he was from. After further conversation, Jean found out what happened to Chogan's father and mother, along with the rest of his village. Chogan told Jean that it was white men who attacked the village because of the horseshoe prints and the empty shell casings, but he did not see who they were. When Jean was done talking to Chogan he explained to everyone what had happened and what brought Chogan there.

"Chogan is Crow, and his village is about a hundred miles north of here, high in the Wind River Range. I don't know how he was able to walk this far. This boy has gone through a terrible experience, and he needs someone to raise him," Jean said.

"That all sounds good and well, but who do you know would be willing to take in a young Indian boy and raise him?" Henry asked.

"Henry, I'll tell you this, I will take him and raise him until I can find someone who will care for him. This way we will have someone that can at least talk to the boy," Jack volunteered.

"That's real decent of you Jack, and if I can help in any way, let me know," Henry replied.

Jack, Jean, and Chogan left the ranch together. Two months had passed with no sign of Chogan or how things were going. One day Henry and Margaret went to town for supplies at the mercantile. Jack happened to be there, buying materials to be made into clothing along with other supplies for Chogan.

"I'm glad I ran into you. You know the Prescotts, they have a large cattle operation about ten miles west of town. They have agreed to take Chogan and give him a permanent home. In fact I am gathering up some things to send with him. Sam Prescott will be by tomorrow to pick up Chogan and take him to the ranch. He has two ranch hands who will be able to talk to Chogan. One of the men is a half-breed, and the other lived among the Sioux for several years," Jack replied.

"I hope everything works out. Otherwise Chogan is going to have a rough life just trying to survive in a white community. Keep me posted," Henry commented.

Five years passed, and Chogan adapted to the Prescott family and ranching. There was still that same recurring feeling about his mother and father and who killed them. It had been on his mind for years, but he was too young to take on the challenge of searching out the killers.

One day Sam asked Chogan to come to the house; there was something he wanted to tell him with the help of one of his ranch hand interpreter. Sam told Chogan that he had decided to send him to the Carlisle Indian Industrial School in Pennsylvania to learn how to speak English and to assimilate into the white man's culture. Chogan did not understand and wanted to stay with the Prescotts. Two weeks later Chogan arrived at the school. He was immediately stripped of his clothing and was ordered to put on clothing furnished by the school. The following day he was ordered to have his hair cut in the style of a young white boy. Chogan was terrified, and he refused to cooperate with the school headmaster. He was punished severely with lashings for not readily accepting the school's policy. He was no longer allowed to speak in his native language and was required to learn and speak English. If he was caught talking to anyone in his native tongue he was lashed by the Head master.

One day Chogan received a letter from Sam, telling him his wife had died of diphtheria. Chogan was greatly saddened by the news. Sam's wife, Lucie, had treated him like a son. Chogan sent a letter expressing his condolences.

Following several years of repeated lashings, Chogan decided to relent and obey his instructors until the time was right for him to escape. Chogan learned to fight and act like a white man; however, he was more determined than ever to avenge the murder of his mother and father. He had been taught the ways of the white man and could speak their language. Now was the right time for him to leave the school.

Late one night after supper, he and other children were allowed to walk around the compound for a short time before returning to their respective rooms. The night was dark with a layer of clouds hiding a full moon. Though Chogan was scared and afraid of the consequences if he was caught running away, he was still determined to return to the Prescott ranch. Two weeks later, after making his way by train and crossing two rivers, he arrived at the ranch. Sam was upset to see Chogan; he thought he should have stayed.

"Mr. Prescott, would you like to know why I left?" Chogan asked.

"I sure would. You know they will be looking for you to take you back," Sam insisted.

Chogan took his shirt off and showed Sam the scars left from several years of lashings.

"My lord, how long had this been going on?" Sam asked.

"For several years, from the day I arrived at the school," Chogan replied.

"I am sorry that you were put in that situation. I understand now why you ran away. Don't worry, if they come looking for you I will not let them take you back," Sam said.

It was easier now that Chogan could speak English and could communicate with everyone on the ranch. Sam and his late wife had two sons. One was named Charles, who was the oldest; the other was named Frank. Both sons were hardheaded and manipulative. Neither was like his father who was an honest hardworking man. The sons were spoiled, and they expected everything be given them.

One evening after everyone had left the supper table, Chogan noticed one of the son's gun belt and holster hanging over a log chair. He removed one of the cartridges and put it in his pocket. Later that night he compared the empty cartridge to the one he removed from the gun belt. They are a match; they were both .46 caliber. This was not a common caliber used by most men. The calibers of choice were generally either .44 or .45. Chogan decided to take the two cartridges to the feed store in town and ask the owner about who uses this caliber of gun. Chogan walked into the store and asked for the owner.

"I am the owner. My name is Mike Corbin. What can I do for you, young man?"

"My name is Chogan, and I live with the Prescott family on their ranch. I want to ask you a question about a certain caliber gun."

"Well, son, ask away."

"Mr. Corbin, who do you know uses a .46 caliber gun? I have never seen this caliber before," Chogan asked as he took the cartridges out of his pocket and handed them over to Mr. Corbin.

"Where did you get these?" Mr. Corbin asked.

"Why does that matter? I just want to know if anyone around here uses this caliber of cartridge."

"Well, I guess it really doesn't matter, son. I know of only two people that use .46 caliber revolvers. They would be the sons of Sam Prescott."

"Thanks, Mr. Corbin, you've been a great help. It's only a matter of life and death," Chogan shouted as he ran out the door.

"Wait a minute, what do you mean by that?" Mike Corbin yelled.

Chogan ran to his horse and rode off without saying another word. There was little question in Chogan's mind as to who raided his village and killed his mother and father. There were others involved, but he had no way of knowing whether or not they were still in this part of the country because the massacre took place many years ago.

Mike Corbin ran out the door and down the street to the sheriff's office. Out of breath, Mike said, "Harve, something terrible is going to happen. You need to ride out to that Prescott ranch right away!" Mike told the sheriff what Chogan said before riding off in a hurry.

"I'm not sure it means anything. You shouldn't worry about things until something happens," replied the sheriff.

"That's what I'm afraid of! What if something happens when Chogan gets back to the ranch? Sheriff, you need to ride out to the Prescott ranch just in case there is trouble," Mike said.

"All right, I'll ride out and see if anything is going on. Meanwhile, I suggest you get back to your store before someone robs you!" Harve said in a laughing way.

Chogan had arrived back at the ranch and was walking up the stairs to the main entrance when the sheriff rode up and yelled, "Wait a minute, son, I will go inside with you."

Chogan stopped on the porch and waited for the sheriff to catch up.

"Please come in, Sheriff, I'm glad you're here. There is a serious matter that needs to be discussed with Mr. Prescott," Chogan said.

Sam walked out of the parlor and saw Chogan and the sheriff standing in the hallway.

"What brings you out this way, Harve? I haven't had the pleasure for a long time," Sam asked.

"Actually, Sam, I don't really know other than Mike Corbin came running down the street into my office and said there might be trouble between you and Chogan."

"Sheriff, I'm not aware of any problems between us. Let's ask Chogan. Well, Chogan, what in the world is going on? I thought you were happy here. Have we mistreated you in any way? I thought you wanted to become part of the Prescott heritage," Sam said in a surprised voice.

"Mr. Prescott, I appreciate everything you have done more for me, but I do have a serious matter to discuss with you and your sons," Chogan replied.

"Do you want to talk to me about the concerns first, or shall I have Charles and Frank join us?" Sam asked.

"I would feel better with everyone here, including the sheriff," Chogan replied.

Sam stood up and walked to outside and yelled for Pedro, one of his hands, to have his sons come to the ranch house immediately. After both sons returned they both began complaining about being interrupted while there was still daylight.

"Just shut up and sit down and don't say another word until I tell you to," Sam remarked angrily. "Go ahead, Chogan, and say what's on your mind now that you have everyone stirred up," Sam continued.

"Mr. Prescott, do you remember the first time I came here? You caught me blowing a whistle and asked me what I was doing, but I didn't understand! I was blowing on a .46 caliber cartridge shell that I found on the ground following the attack of my father and mother and the rest of my people. It took me several years to question who might have murdered my people. You see in my hand, an empty cartridge I found on the ground following the massacre. I never thought much about it and just used it for a whistle. This was one of several empty cartridges scattered around.

"I saw something else, horseshoe prints made by shod horses ridden by white men, not Indian ponies. One set of prints looked like a letter *S* had been stamped into the shoe. After thinking about everything, I decided to find out who uses a .46 caliber gun and if any of the horses here had the same stamped imprint. After checking around I found that all the horses on the ranch have the same stamped imprint. I took my cartridge to Mr. Corbin's store and asked him who uses a .46 caliber pistol. He told me there were only two people that he knew of, and they were Mr. Prescott's sons. I want to know if either son killed my father and mother at my village several years ago," Chogan explained.

"We don't have to sit here and listen to a filthy Indian accusing us of something that happened years ago. Other people use .46 caliber guns. It could have been anyone," Frank said.

Sam stood up and backhanded Frank, knocking him off his chair.

"You disgust me," Sam said.

"That's right, Dad, he has no proof of anything. Who do you believe, your sons or an Indian you want to raise?" Charles said angrily.

"Both of you, shut your mouths! You need to show some respect around here. Chogan has become a part of this family in spite of the two of you. Ever since your mother passed away you two have been nothing but a pain in my side. I don't ever want to hear either of you talk about Chogan in this manner again, do you understand?" Sam shouted.

"Yes, sir," both sons replied.

"Now it's my turn to ask the questions, and you two had better not lie to me. Were you a part of the killings that day at the Crow village?" Sam asked.

Frank turned to his brother and said, "Of course we weren't there. We have never been to that part of the country."

"As I recall, the two of you along with some of the boys from the Flying D went elk hunting in the Wind River Range about the time of the killings."

"We had no part in the killings. We only went along with the others. It was Jamie Young's idea," Charles said out of fear.

"Shut up, Charles, we agreed to say nothing about this to anyone," Frank said in a concerned voice.

The sheriff spoke up, "I believe I have heard enough. I am going to have to take you boys in to stand trial for murder."

"Dad, you have to believe us, we didn't kill anyone! Please don't let the sheriff take us in," Charles begged.

"I don't know what to believe—that you two have been lying to me for years, and maybe it's time you stand up like men and take your punishment," Sam replied. The sheriff had cuffed the two boys before leaving for town.

Chogan asked, "What will happen to them if they are found guilty, Mr. Prescott?"

"They will probably hang," Sam replied as he placed his head in his hands. "I'll have no one after they are gone. I must not have been a very good father, or things might have turned out differently."

"Mr. Prescott, I believe we all need to know what happened to my people that day. I am sorry your sons were mixed up in this. I thought of killing them both without talking to you first, but I could not. You have treated me like a son, and out of respect, I just couldn't go through with it," Chogan said.

"The sad part about this whole situation is that you have turned out better than my sons, and I will always love you in the same way," Sam said.

The trial was set for two weeks, allowing time for the circuit judge to arrive. There was a jury selection of nine men. The day of the trial had finally come. It seemed like an eternity for the two sons who were scared to death of being found guilty and hanged. Early that morning the two men were escorted to the general store where the trial would take place. Everyone for miles around had heard of the trial and wanted to see it firsthand. The room over flowed with men, women, and children curious to see the outcome.

The court was in session, and it lasted most of the day with the majority of questions coming from the defense attorney. As the session continued it became clear that Frank and Charles were as much a part of the killings as anyone else. After testimony of both sides the prosecutor rested his case, and the jury was taken to a private room across the street in the hotel. After four hours of deliberation the jurors returned to announce the verdict. Before the jurors were given time to announce the verdict the judge asked if anyone would like to say anything on behalf of the two sons. Chogan raised his hand and asked to speak.

"Go ahead, young man. State your name and reason for your comments," the judge ordered.

"Your Honor, my name is Chogan. I believe most everyone knows who I am. I have been raised by Mr. Prescott and have been treated as well as anyone could. It is true, I am the one who initiated the charges against the two sons of Mr. Prescott. I believe anyone in this room would have done the same thing I have done—finding the answer to who killed my father and mother. It is not my desire to seek retribution, only knowledge of what happened and who was involved. Hanging two men who made a mistake several years ago won't bring back the dead. I do not want to press charges at this time. I wish to withdraw all charges for everyone's sake. There has been enough heartache and suffering on both sides. I am asking for the mercy of the court to release Charles and Frank and dismiss all charges. Thank you all for listening to me."

"I believe Chogan touched the hearts of everyone present. In view of what has happened and the appeal to the court, I am dismissing all charges," the judge said.

After the court adjourned, Sam walked over to Chogan and his sons. "I would like everyone to return to the ranch for I have something important to tell everyone." Upon returning to the ranch Sam asked everyone to come into the parlor. After everyone was seated he began to speak.

"This day has been both a great relief and a tragedy. I have lost two sons and have gained another. I have made a hard decision to eliminate both of you—Charles and Frank—from my will. I have decided to replace the two of you with Chogan, to whom everything will go upon my death. I want you boys to gather all your personal belongings and leave immediately. You may leave on the horses you have been riding. I don't ever want to hear from either of you as long as I'm alive. I have one son, and he will remain with me here throughout the rest of my life."

DEVIL'S RANGE

The year was 1870 in Abilene, Kansas. Gathered around the bar in the Cattleman's Saloon, Matt Fraser began telling a story of what happened to him and other men who were part of the once infamous cattle drive crossing the Devil's Range. The drive began outside Dallas where Tom Jeffrey, the owner of the split horn ranch, offered every drover $60.00 and the trail bosses $150.00 a month to take the five thousand head of Texas longhorns across Texas leading through the Devil's Range rather than riding around it. This would shorten the drive by about two months, leading the herd onto the railhead at Abilene.

"Since this cattle drive was so dangerous, double pay was offered to each of us. Sixty drovers and two trail bosses were hired that day. The herd was divided in two. Twenty men rode on each side, with twenty riding down the middle dividing the herd. Four men rode point, and another four rode drag. This was to keep the herd together at all times, keeping strays to a minimum."

Legend preceded the cattle drive for many years; anyone crossing into the Devil's Range would not return. The story was based on many of the great Indian warriors making a deal with the Devil, allowing them to roam and live much like each of them had prior to death; in exchange, each agreed to do the Devil's work by keeping his range free of anyone.

The first week out was calm with no serious problems. The second week a storm started to move in, so the cattle were kept in a tight formation in case of lightning. The last thing anyone wanted was a stampede. The sky grew darker, and the windswept rain began making it impossible to keep watch over the herd. The lightning began, followed by the crack of thunder; the herd began to stampede.

Everyone was awakened, and they mounted up in efforts to keep the herd together. In the course of the night two men riding inside were thrown and trampled to death. One of the chuck wagons overturned, and the cook was seriously injured, leaving both legs crushed. The cook was slowly removed from beneath the wagon and taken to the stream and propped up against the bank. It was already too late, he was dead. He was buried in a shallow grave, and then the contents of the one wagon were loaded onto the other. The bottom of each chuck wagon contained two compartments each that stored guns and ammo in case of an emergency.

Hours later the storm began to let up. The herd had been rounded up, and a count was taken. In addition to the two dead men two others were gone.

"No one just disappears in this country," Jed Aikens, one of the trail bosses, said.

"Tomorrow, you three men," as Jed pointed, "will look for the two drovers."

At sunup the next day the riders set out.

Following along a steam, one of the riders yelled out, "Over here! I found something!" The other two rode over to where the rider was.

One of the men climbed down from his horse and walked over to a dead man's body then rolled the man over to see who it was.

"Who is it?" one of the men shouted.

"It's Russ Turley. There's something strange going on here, he has been scalped." There had been so sign of Indians at all.

"We need to look for the other man," another drover said.

The three riders spread out along the stream looking on both sides. Suddenly a man was spotted setting up against a small cottonwood. The rider climbed down from his horse, cautiously approaching the man. The man appeared to be staring straight ahead.

The rider asked, "Mister, are you all right?" There was no answer. As he walked closer he realized the man was Streck Shephard and was dead. After pulling him away from the tree, he noticed he had two arrows broken off in his back; his body fell to the ground. The other men had caught up with the rider.

"What is going on here? I have never seen anything like this. Two men killed by Indians none of us have seen?"

Later that day everyone gathered around the chuck wagon to discuss what had happened and what should be done. Nerves were on edge, as if they were being pursued by phantoms no one could see. It was too late to turn back. The herd would be on the Devil's Range for several more weeks.

The other trail boss, Jed, spoke up, "You can't drive a herd this size filled with fear. We need to discuss the situation logically. First of all, we are going to double every task. There will be eight men riding drag and eight riding point. If you see any sign of Indians or anything unusual, don't fire a shot. Send one of you back to camp as a messenger. We can't afford to lose another man. I want night watch to be doubled with fewer men riding in the middle of the herd. I don't want anyone out of sight of anyone else, do you understand? It could be a matter of life or death."

Each one shouted yes or nodded in agreement. The following day was uneventful with no losses of livestock or lives. Later that evening the valley narrowed, leaving a canyon on the east side of the trail. There were thirty men on the canyon side making sure the herd didn't stray over the side. Dusk settled in, and the herd was calm. In the distance you could hear an occasional whine of a coyote.

Suddenly in the shadows one of the riders saw a ghostly image of a warrior riding between him and the canyon.

He rode ahead and asked the other rider in a low voice if he had noticed anything unusual. He remarked he had seen the same thing.

"If I didn't know better I believe I saw a ghost warrior," the man said.

"We had better keep an eye out and don't stray far away," the other rider said. The next morning everyone assembled around the chuck wagon for breakfast.

"I want to take a head count before head back out," Jed said.

After taking a head count, five more men were missing. "We'd better find out who the five men were and what happened to them," one of the drovers said in a concerned voice.

"Just wait a minute, before everyone panics, we need to change our strategy!" Conn, the other trail boss, shouted. "I want everyone to pull two shifts. This means twenty-four hours on at a time. Somehow we need to get a handle on what's going on. I want you boys," he pointed his hand to several men standing by the fire, "to find out what happened to the missing men, then report back here immediately. You stay together and don't become separated, you understand?"

The men mounted up and rode off toward the canyon rim, searching for the five men. Looking over the side, one of the riders noticed several head of cattle and what looked like three bodies lying at the bottom of a ravine.

"Over here!" he shouted. "It looks like some of the men are down there as he pointed to the bottom of the ravine."

The six men rode down the steep embankment to reach the three men and livestock. All three men had apparently died from broken necks, along with the cattle, as if they had been driven off the canyon side. The strange thing was that none of the personal belongings of the men had been taken. The cattle were left where they fell; the bodies were left intact. The men tied each of the dead men on the horses and led them back up to the main camp.

"Did you find all five bodies?" Jed asked.

"No, sir, just three bodies along with some of the livestock left in the bottom of the ravine," one of the men explained.

Ted and several of the others walked over to the dead men draped over the horses. After cutting them loose, it was apparent each had died of the fall.

"How many head did we lose?" Jed asked.

One of the men spoke up, "It looked like about a dozen or so. We couldn't tell for sure, some of the cattle were hanging off the rocks. At this rate there won't be enough men to finish the drive." The trail bosses were trying to figure out how they could protect the herd and keep the men safe at the same time.

Conn shook his head. "You know, I've never seen anything like this before. Have you?"

"Me either," Jed replied.

"All I know, we can't afford to lose another man, or this drive will be over!" Jed commented.

"I don't know of anything else we can do," Conn said.

"The only other possibility would be to divide the herd in two and form separate drives. I am not sure this will change anything either," Jed commented.

"Before we do anything else I think we'd better send out some men to scout ahead and find out if there is any way around this situation or how much further until we are off the range," Con said in a bewildered voice.

All the men who could be spared were brought back into camp to discuss the plan.

"Men, what we are going to do is we are sending four of you ahead to scout the region and to determine if there is another way out of here or how much longer until we get off the range. Henry, hand me your hat. Ted, pull out a deck of playing card, shuffle them then place them in the hat. Each of you will draw a card. The face cards will count as they are—the jack, queen, and king will be ranked accordingly. In the event of drawing the same card the highest suit will determine the man in. The ace is a wild card, allowing that man to leave if he chooses. Does everyone understand the rules? It could be a matter of life or death!"

The men all nodded. The cards were drawn, and the four men prepared to leave.

"Oh, one more thing. If none of you returns we won't be sending out a search party. You will be on your own. We wish you Godspeed!"

The next morning before dawn, the four riders left the camp, riding north. They decided to stay together as long as possible. The remainder of that day was peaceful with no major problems. The next morning they rode to a high point and surveyed the countryside for a possible better way. The problem is without water, the trail drive would be doomed. The men determined it would be at least two more weeks before the drive would take them out of the hostile land.

At this time they decided to split up, leaving in opposite directions for one day to explore other options.

They agreed to meet back at the same departure point the end the next day and decide where to go from there.

The next day ended with only two of the four men returning; however, Jack's horse came toward them with something hanging from the saddle horn. As the horse drew closer they could see a blood-soaked rawhide bag hanging down with something sticking out of the top. Pete reached over to untie the bag and saw the top of Jack's head inside. He immediately dropped the bag and jumped down from his horse and started vomiting, heaving until nothing was left inside. Jake, after seeing Jack's head, doubled over in the saddle and cried. There was no explanation for what they witnessed.

"Why would anyone do something this terrible to anyone?"

"Well, partner, I guess we had better ride back and join the herd," Pete said.

Jake and Pete mounted up, riding back to meet the slow-moving herd. Two days later they caught up.

"Look!" one of the men shouted. "Someone is coming this way."

After riding closer everyone could see the extra horse with the bloody bag hanging off the saddle horn.

"We made it back, but you may not want to see this." Jake pointed to the bloody bag that was starting to dry out. Many of the drovers rode back to camp to hear the news. After finding out what happed to Jack, Jed and Conn were more worried than ever. Jared didn't return at all; no one knew for sure what happened to him.

"Well, men, what do you think we should do?" Conn asked.

Jake spoke up, "I think whatever we do we don't want to go east. Just stay on course or maybe head west."

Pete said, "We did not find water going west, but we only rode out one day before returning."

Jed turned to Conn and said, "I think we have ridden into hell, and we need to find our way out!"

"Instead of driving a herd of cattle across this country, we are being hunted down by an enemy we can't see or find."

"We need to get out of here as fast as possible before we lose many more men or cattle," Jed replied.

"I believe you're right. I think we should move the herd to the west and hope we find water and cut our losses," Conn replied.

Word was sent to all the outriders, letting them know at sunup they would be heading west rather to continue north. The next morning everyone saddled up and formed the cattle in a straight line, heading them due west. After all day, there was no sign of water, and some of the cattle were beginning to dehydrate. This meant they would lose much of the weight that had been gained along the way, bringing less at the market.

"We have to find water nearby or we will all die along with the cattle. I will leave with one of the drovers and look for water and be back before nightfall. I know it is risky, but we have no choice," Jed said in a strong voice.

"I don't like your plan one bit, but I don't have a better one," Conn replied.

Jed grabbed one of the drovers, asking him to ride along. After riding over fifteen miles, they finally came across a small stream. The cattle would have to be led to the stream in shifts as the bank was small and wouldn't hold many at one time. It would be too risky to spread the cattle out up and down the stream; rather, they wanted to keep them bunched up. The men rode from a long day's ride, barely able to find their way back to the camp before dark. As dawn approached, something strange was noticed on the west side of the trail. There appeared to be several small fires that had been lit running north as far as the eye could see. What did this mean? Someone set these fires to prevent the herd from being driven west, forcing them to stay on the Devil's Range.

Jed spoke up, "I don't think we have any choice but to drive the herd through the fire breaks leading to the west. We must keep them as tightly together as possible to minimize our losses. If we are forced to continue north, we will be sitting ducks. We can take a vote. It's each man's choice. Don't forget we are on our last barrel of water, and the cattle are going to die within the next few days if nothing changes."

After some discussion attitudes flared, but in the end, it was a unanimous choice to go through the fire breaks and take a chance. The drive took a westerly course. As the herd came closer to the fire breaks, it was if there was little or no room to herd them through without burning to death. They had no choice but to continue north until they reached a point in the breaks where they could push the cattle through.

Five miles later came the opportunity to turn the cattle back west.

The men stampeded them through the fire breaks, heading them toward the small stream on the other side.

Many of the cattle refused to go through the fire and died in their tracks while others, out of extreme fear, went ahead anyway. This would be the worst day of the drive. The loss of cattle was in excess of eight hundred head along with ten more men. The drive had taken its toll, losing over 10 percent of the herd and about one-third of the drovers. After the hard day's drive, they finally reached the stream where they watered the cattle in shifts until the herd was refreshed.

Everyone was at his wits end; no one could endure another day like this one. The unexpected had created a level of fear that made the strongest tremble, starting to impact each man's performance. Since the stream ran to the north, they decided to continue west, taking the herd farther away from the Devil's Range. The next two days were as they should be with no particular difficulties.

The following morning it began to rain. As the drive continued the driving rain became worse, blinding the trail and unexpectedly pushing the herd into a box canyon. The rain began to let up, but sunset was rapidly approaching, leaving little time to assess the situation. Leading into the canyon was a stream that was now swollen because of the torrential downpour, creating another problem and requiring the cattle to be taken to higher ground out of the flood area.

"Okay, boys, let's move 'em out of here to higher land!" Conn shouted.

The men were near exhaustion, but they knew the cattle could not be left in the canyon. The men formed a circle behind the herd and the canyon wall, slowly pushing the herd forward to the opening of the box canyon and out of the flood area. By the time the cattle were safe the men grabbed their bed rolls, laid them on the soaked ground, collapsed on them in their wet ponchos, and fell asleep.

After everyone had fallen asleep a roar above the canyon could be heard. It was getting louder and louder. Everyone was now backing up; they were looking at the canyon walls around them, which were beginning to fall away because of the intense rain. The canyon walls on three sides would soon reach the stream and would cause it to flood toward the opening where the cattle had been bedded down but an hour before, potentially causing a landslide downstream. There was no time to waste; everyone would have to drag out their overworked bodies and move everything out of the canyon entrance. By the time everyone awakened and mounted up the rush of water had already flowed over the temporary dam created by the falling cliffs. It was beginning to overtake the men and the herd. Each man was now on his own, trying to save his own life.

"The herd had to be abandoned. Men had been thrown from their horse, and many were attempting to claw their way up the steep embankment, away from the carnage below. Two days later, the remains of the herd and the men slowly wandered into a small town west of Abilene. Jed, I, and six other were the only survivors. No one knows how many cattle made it through. Following a day of rest we finally made our way to Abilene where Jed sent a telegram to Tom Jeffrey, explaining the tragedy. Within two days, three thousand dollars had been wired to Jed to be distributed to the rest of us. Shortly afterwards we heard Tom had taken his life, after having lost everything."

The men left standing around the bar were so emotionally drained they left without uttering a word.

ENSENADA

The day was hot, with draught-like conditions across Yuma into Mexico. The land had seen no rain for over a month. Sarah Butler had waited for as long as she could before riding to Yuma on business.

The ride was too hard on her horse; there was nowhere to water him between the small ranch north of town and Yuma. Sarah had waited for a cooler day to ride into town. She desperately needed to borrow money to keep the ranch. Sarah was behind on her mortgage to Sam Slotter, an attorney holding the deed. She knew he was ready to foreclose if she didn't come up with two hundred dollars by the end of the week. In addition, her crops had failed because of the draught. She had neither seed nor money to purchase any. Sarah had worked the land for seven years, trying to build up a small herd and raise some crops. Her husband ran off with an old friend who showed up one day. Neither was ever seen again.

She was forced to sell off all but two head of livestock to pay for hay for what remained and food for her. If the bank would not loan her enough money to bring her mortgage current and to buy feed and other necessary supplies, she would lose everything.

Sarah mounted up and left before dawn. Yuma was about twenty-five mile from her ranch. It would be a good day's ride. It was the middle of the afternoon when Sarah came across an old stone building whose walls had fallen to hard times many years before. Sarah stopped to rest and get both her and her horse out of the heat before riding on. She sought shelter behind one of the stone walls that was still standing, blocking out the sun. She had to reach Yuma and the bank before it closed. Sarah pushed her horse as fast as she could in fear he could die of the heat. She was running out of time; the bank would close in the next few minutes, and she would be forced to wait until the next day to complete her business. Sarah pushed her horse to near exhaustion before reaching town. She climbed down and tied the horse up behind the bank. Sarah began walking around the front when she heard a voice inside.

"Keep your hands up, and no one will get hurt," came a voice from inside the bank.

Sarah stopped on the boardwalk in front of the bank; looking through a window, she saw a man with a scarf-covered face backing toward the front door of the bank with two saddlebags bulging with money. This so happened to be the opportunity Sarah needed.

Without further thought she waited for the holdup man to back outside through the door with gun in hand, ready to shoot anyone trying to stop him. In that moment Sarah made a decision that would change her life forever. After the man was outside Sarah drew her pistol from beneath her flowing skirt and told the man to drop his gun, or she would shoot.

"Who are you?" the man shouted.

"It doesn't matter who I am, mister. Just drop those saddlebags and kick them over to me!" Sarah shouted.

"Okay!"

Sarah bent down and removed the money from each bag and kicked the saddlebags back to the outlaw.

"Now, mister, take those saddlebags and get on your horse and get out of here before I change my mind."

The man turned and said, "They will kill me if I try to leave now!"

"It's your call. Either I shoot you right here, or you take your chances."

The bank robber grabbed the two saddlebags and ran for his horse, which was tied up in front of the bank.

Sarah yelled "It's a holdup!" before disappearing around the corner that led to her horse in the rear of the bank. The holdup man was on his horse, kicking it in the side and trying to leave town as fast as he could. Everyone in the bank rushed outside to see what was happening.

Lon Schaeffer, the sheriff, ran out on to Main Street and shot at the bank robber. The second shot hit the man, knocking him off his horse and to the ground. By now several of the townspeople saw what happened and ran over to where the man was lying on the ground. The sheriff reached the man first.

Looking down on the injured man, the sheriff asked, "Who are you?"

The man tried to say something, but it was too late; he was gone.

"Hand me those saddlebags!" the sheriff yelled. One of the men standing there picked up the saddlebags and handed them to the sheriff.

The sheriff opened both of them. There was nothing inside.

"Is this some kind of a joke? There is no money inside!" the sheriff shouted. "This was the man that robbed the bank. Money doesn't just walk away! What happened, did anyone see anyone take the money from the saddlebags?"

The bank president stepped forward. "This is the man who held us up. I'm not sure how much he got away with, but it was over twelve thousand dollars. We'll have to tally up the losses and let you know."

The sheriff yelled out again, "Did anyone see anyone else with the dead man?"

No one answered; several people just nodded no.

Sarah was riding as fast as her horse could take her back to her ranch. She knew that in time the sheriff and his men would figure out that she may have taken the money. Once she reached the ranch she decided to take a few of her personal belongings and ride toward Mexico. Sarah had no time to think about anything. She had a lot of cash, and in that moment of desperation, she had to do whatever was necessary to avoid being caught by the law. After seven days of hard riding Sarah arrived in the small lazy town of Ensenada. Ensenada was in Mexico, about two hundred miles south of Yuma. It was a dusty little town with adobe buildings lining the main street. People were walking around not paying attention to her or anyone. Sarah stopped in front of a livery stable and asked a man where she could stay and get a good meal.

"My name is Luis and the best place to stay and eat is the El Centro," he pointed across the street.

"I want to leave my horse here for the night. How much will it cost me, Louise?"

"It will be twenty five cents a day, and the feed is another twenty five cents for hay and oats, ma'am."

"That sounds fine. Here's fifty cents, and I will be back tomorrow to get my horse," Sarah said.

That evening in her room Sarah counted the money. She had twelve thousand five hundred dollars and seventy-five cents. Sarah kept the money stashed in the saddlebags and several pockets in her flared skirt.

The next morning Sarah asked around about any ranches for sale. A man at the bar of the hotel overheard the conversation and interrupted Sarah and the barkeeper.

"I couldn't help but hear you talking about buying a ranch in the area, and I know of one or two for sale. Please let me introduce myself. My name is LaRocha Mestas, and I deal in such matters."

"Mr. Mestas, I am interested in buying a small ranch hereabouts."

"If I may ask, how much do you have to spend on such an investment?"

"It depends on the size, the water rights, and the number of livestock included. I would be willing to pay up to five thousand dollars for the right place."

Two weeks had passed since the bank holdup, and the sheriff was still puzzled about what happened to the money. One morning while sitting at his desk a young woman came into his office.

"What can I do for you, miss?" the sheriff asked.

"I'm not sure, Sheriff, but I have been thinking about what happened when the bank was held up. And I didn't want to say anything, but the more I thought about it, the more I felt I needed to tell you something."

"Well, just spit it out. What is it you want to tell me miss?"

"That evening after the bank robbery, I was walking towards the laundry house when I saw a woman with long hair come around the corner of the bank and climb on her horse and rode off in a hurry. Kind of as if she was running away or something. As I think back it seemed kind of strange."

"Why didn't you speak out before? This is very important information which could help lead to the person who ended up with the holdup money."

"Honestly, Sheriff, it didn't seem that important at the time until I gave it more thought. I guess didn't want to get anyone in trouble."

"Thank you for your time and information. If you think of anything else, please let me know."

The sheriff and his deputy rode out to Sarah's ranch to look for anything that may tie her to the bank holdup. After looking around for a couple of hours they found nothing that would indicate Sarah's involvement in the bank holdup or the money taken. The fact that Sarah had left most of her personal belongings at the ranch along with the two head of livestock that were in desperate need of food and water was puzzling.

"I don't know if Sarah just ran off or if something happened to her," the sheriff said to his deputy.

"It doesn't look like she's been here for several days," the deputy said.

The next day Sam Slotter, an attorney, dropped by the sheriff's office.

"Lon, have you been to Sarah Butler's ranch?" he asked.

"Yes, why do you ask? My deputy and I were out there yesterday looking for clues that may tie Sarah to the bank holdup, but we found nothing."

"I don't know if you were aware of the fact that I hold the deed on Sarah's ranch, and she is past due two hundred dollars. I told her I was ready to foreclose if she didn't come up with the money two weeks ago. I haven't heard nor seen anything of her since then."

"So, Sam, what are your plans now that Sarah has disappeared?"

"I plan to file the necessary paperwork and start foreclosure proceedings against Sarah and the property."

"By way of curiosity, how much does Sarah owe on the property?"

"It is somewhere around twenty two hundred dollars," Sam replied.

"Who do you think will pay that for that rundown, weed-ridden place?" the sheriff asked.

"I don't know, but I will soon find out. I'm filing the paper work today, then once I get through the legal process I plan to put it on the market."

"Good luck, Sam!" the sheriff shouted.

In Ensenada, Sarah told LaRocha that before she did any business with him he would need to do something for her.

"But of course! I am here at your service, ma'am. What is it that you would like me to do for you?" LaRocha asked.

"I want you to ride to Yuma and find out what is going on with my ranch. I would like to buy it back, either out of foreclosure or afterwards—which ever I can," Sarah said.

"I thought you wanted to buy a ranch here, not where you came from?" LaRocha asked.

"I want to own two ranches, one here and the other one in Arizona. I will give you five hundred dollars to make the trip and find out all you can. I will give you half up front. You must report back to me in ten days. If not, the deal is off, and I will owe you nothing else."

"I will do this for you but only because you are so beautiful and will be doing business with me," LaRocha replied. The next day LaRocha left town, riding toward Yuma.

Two days out, he was confronted by Mexican bandits.

"Hey, hombre, stop! We would like to talk to you," one of the men yelled.

LaRocha kicked his horse in the flanks and started to run away. One of the bandits shot his horse out from underneath him. LaRocha flew over his horse's head, landing on the hard ground. He knew these men were serious. They wanted everything he had; they weren't there to talk.

"Amigo, we only want your money, your clothes, and everything else," one of the bandits said as he laughed.

LaRocha could barely talk; he was battered from the fall. One of the bandits started to undress him; another pulled his boots off.

"Look here, the man has lots of money. I wonder if there is more where this came from," one of the bandits shouted as he removed the cash from the saddlebags. Two of the men rolled LaRocha over on his stomach and slashed his back.

"This should slow him down," one of the bandits said, laughing as he spoke.

LaRocha screamed in pain as the blood gushed down his back. The bandits mounted up and rode off, leaving LaRocha for dead. LaRocha spotted a small stream nearby and crawled toward it. Once he reached the streams edge, he slowly backed down into the cool water. It had a soothing effect on his back. He still had to stop the bleeding. After spending time in the water, he decided to climb out and look for something to place on his back for protection and to help absorb the blood from the slashes. The only thing he could find were leaves that were lying on the ground. He crawled over to them and rolled on his back atop the leaves. Afterward, he attempted to stand up, hoping that some of the leaves were sticking to the open wounds on his back. It was working; many the leaves were sticking to the slashed areas on his back, sealing off the wounds.

LaRocha stayed close to the water, out of sight for the next two days. He was well enough to start walking back to Ensenada, but he stayed off the main road; he was naked and was still afraid. LaRocha was walking toward Ensenada when he heard many riders coming up from behind. He stepped back into a wooded area waiting to see who they were. It was the Federales. He was happy to see them; he stepped back on the main road, yelling for them to stop. After explaining what happened to him they took him back to Ensenada in one of the supply wagons. Two days later he arrived back in Ensenada. After explaining to Sarah what happened, she decided to wait.

*   *   *

One year later the Yuma mayor and the other board members had a meeting and decided to terminate Lon Schaeffer, the sheriff, because he had failed to find the holdup money that was taken from the bank.

Lon begged for more time to find out what happened to the money, but it was too late; the board had made their decision, and it was final.

Lon experienced many nights of lost sleep over the bank holdup and what happened to the money every night since it took place. Now it was more than a job; it was personal. The nightmare became a reality! Lon was filled with rage; he wanted to be vindicated on his lack of performance.

Lon decided to pursue the matter on his own hands. Someone took the money the day of the holdup, and he would find out who it was if it took him the rest of his life. Lon rode out to Sarah Butler's old dilapidated ranch and scouted around for any clues that would lead him to the money. Sarah had left—apparently for good, as most of her personal belongings were still in the house as she had left them. Nothing was out of order; left on the small wooden table sat dried hardened beans in a tin pan, as if someone had to leave in a hurry. Sarah was the only person Lon knew that remotely fit the description of the woman riding off following the bank robbery. If Sarah left for Mexico, it was out his jurisdiction. But not now; Lon was able to ride into Mexico or anywhere else.

After leaving Sarah's ranch, Lon rode west along the border until he reached the small town of Tecate. Lon inquired around about a woman fitting Sarah's description, but no one had seen nor heard of her. After spending two days in Tecate he decided to continue south toward Ensenada. Sarah had either gone to the coast or into Mexico. She had to be the thief; nothing else made any sense.

Back in Ensenada, Sarah had recently met and married a wealthy Mexican rancher named Miguel Gonzales. She decided to forget about trying to buy her ranch back. She was happy and comfortable in her new surroundings. Sarah's new husband was a fine man and was part of an old aristocratic family representing several generations of wealthy ranchers. Sarah was living the kind of life she had always dreamed of. She was happier than she had been in years, enjoying ranch life and the beauty of Mexico.

One afternoon Miguel and Sarah rode into town so that Sarah could pick up some new material for a dress that she had been waiting for from St. Louis. They had gone over to the cantina to enjoy food and drinks before going back to the ranch. Lon had made his way to Ensenada and happened to be sitting across the room when he saw Sarah and her husband entered the cantina.

Lon looked up and shouted, "Is that you Sarah?"

Sarah turned around and saw Lon sitting in front of a window across the room.

"Who is the man?" Miguel asked Sarah.

"Oh, he is no one of importance. He is the sheriff of Yuma," Sarah replied.

Sarah asked in a loud tone, "What brings you to Ensenada, Sheriff?"

"I was looking for you. I am still trying to find out who took the money off the dead man who robbed the bank!"

"That was a long time ago, and it has nothing to do with me," Sarah said.

"I don't believe you. I think you were the one who stole the money from the robber before I shot him," the sheriff replied.

"Now, mister, if you are accusing my wife of something, you have no jurisdiction here. This isn't Yuma," Miguel shouted.

"I know you stole the money, and you know what it cost me?"

"I have no idea what you are talking about, Sheriff. You are in the wrong place to be accusing me of anything," Sarah said in a boisterous tone.

"Mister, you need to leave before you are carried out of here," Miguel said.

"I'm not leaving until I know the truth. I lost my badge over the bank holdup, and I know you had something to do with it!" Lon shouted.

Miguel motioned for some of the men to throw Lon out of the cantina. Lon drew his gun but was shot by the barkeeper, but before falling to the floor, he shot Sarah. They both lied dead on the floor in the cantina. The sheriff's question was unanswered, and Sarah never had to explain to her husband about the bank holdup and how she came by the money.

FORSAKEN

Laura and Dever Ingstrom had made their way from Philadelphia, leaving behind their worldly possessions, which had been either sold or auctioned off. With great reluctance and sadness they each left their families behind as well before finally arriving in St. Louis, Missouri, several weeks later. Their dream was to go west and eventually settle in the Willamette Valley region of Oregon. They were to meet a wagon train heading west. In addition to everything they sold, they had managed to save over five hundred dollars to pay for two passages on the wagon train.

Dever and Laura married young and were dreamers. Laura was a frail woman who had been taken care of by her older sister since she was a small child. Laura and Dever's decisions were poor; they never seemed to learn from their mistakes. It didn't matter they had decided together to go west having been told of the perils that could face them. They were blinded by adventure and the promise of a new land, where they could put their roots down and raise a family and have something of their own. One morning Laura complained about feeling sick and throwing up.

"You need to see a doctor before we leave. Let's make sure you are up to the travel," Dever said. An appointment was set with a local doctor. Following his examination, he told Laura that she was pregnant and that she should rest for a while before considering making such an arduous trip.

"How far along am I?" Laura asked the doctor.

"You are at least four months and possibly five months along," the doctor replied.

Dever asked, "How could that be, Laura? Surely you would have known?"

The doctor commented, "I have never examined a woman that didn't know she was pregnant, especially this far along."

"What are we going to do now?" Dever asked.

"We are going to go anyway," Laura replied.

"I don't think that is a good idea. You need to rest for some time before taking on that kind of physical activity. You could jeopardize your pregnancy along with your own life!" the doctor suggested.

"Laura, maybe we should cancel the trip and wait until next year," Dever suggested.

"I won't have any part of it. We will begin tomorrow as planned!"

They were loading up their wagon, preparing for the journey the next day. The wagons were loaded on steamships traveling two hundred miles upstream on the Missouri River before heading north to Independence, Missouri, where they would be unloaded and transferred to wagons. This is when the hard work will begin. The journey would take about six months and would cover about two thousand miles, taking them to the Willamette Valley in Oregon—provided that everything went as planned.

After the wagons were unloaded, the wagon master met with everyone, giving them detailed instructions before crossing the Great Plains. He told everyone to stay together and not to wander off during the day. There were no landmarks, and a person could become lost in a matter of minutes.

The water and food had to be rationed to ensure every man, woman, and child would have sufficient nourishment.

There were twenty wagons making up Laura and Devers's train. On a good day the wagons could travel about ten miles. Some days, they were lucky to make two to three miles, depending on the weather. This time of year the weather was cool with spring rains cooling the prairie. The nights were chilly with everyone sitting around the camp fire.

Over the next few weeks everyone became acquainted with some developing friendships, some lasting a life time. This gave everyone a chance to share their dreams and tell everyone about their families and where they came from. Following a short stay in Omaha, which allowed everyone to rest up and replenish supplies the journey continued across Nebraska.

Laura had weathered the journey well to this point; however, she was annoyed by the wind, the rain, and the mosquitos. She had never been exposed to these elements before, and she looked for Dever to take care of everything.

"Laura, I can't control the weather or the mosquitos," Dever said.

"I know you can't, but I can't stand everything happening at the same time, that's all."

The next leg of the journey would take them across the Great Plains away from all civilization. Day after day of tedious walking or riding in the covered wagon, Laura was in tears. She had no one to talk to other than those on the train and Dever. She started to miss her family and friends.

"I don't know how much longer I can continue! I am sick and tired of seeing nothing but this endless prairie and facing the wind every day!" Laura yelled.

"You need to calm down, we have just begun our journey and you are losing control already. What's going to happen in a couple of months if this keeps up?" Dever asked.

It was obvious that Laura's nerves were starting to fray, and if this kept up, the trip would be a disaster. The wagon train was two weeks out of Omaha when one afternoon a band of Indians approached the wagons wanting something. The wagon master rode out to the chief and asked him what he wanted. The chief said his people needed meat, which they had not eaten in over two weeks, and the squaws and children had become weakened.

The wagon master told the chief that they had no meat to spare and that they needed everything they had to sustain the people for at least another week. The wagon master offered the chief some flour and potatoes to help his people get by. This was not acceptable, and the chief rode away stirring up dust in a fit of anger. Laura saw what had happened and went running out after the chief shouting something. Suddenly the chief turned around and rode back toward Laura as fast as he could, suddenly stopping in front of her, throwing dirt in her face. Three men from the wagon train along with Laura's husband ran toward her with guns in hand. The wagon master said not to shoot and that the chief was just mad. Dever took Laura back to the camp and tried to comfort her.

She was not suited for the journey and would have to be taken back. The problem was the wagon train was too far along for anyone to leave and go back alone through hostile country. Dever was concerned about Laura's mental state and her pregnancy. The next three days the wagon train pushed west against heavy winds and torrential rains. They had traveled less than twenty miles in the three days.

The wagon train was already one week behind, with some concern about winter setting in early. There was no place on the plains or in the mountains to stop, or everyone could perish. With each passing day Laura appeared weakened physically and mentally; she was experiencing exhaustion, especially with the baby and all. Dever asked several of the other women to watch over Laura and let him know if they noticed anything strange happening with her. Late one night, Laura awakened and climbed out of the wagon then started walking north across the prairie, as if she was looking for something.

One of the women spotted her and ran toward her. "Laura, where are you going? You should be in bed. You could miscarry if you're not careful," the woman said.

Laura turned and said, "I am going to visit my daughter. I know she is somewhere out here."

"Your daughter is still inside you. She has not been born yet," the woman explained. The woman put her arms around Laura and slowly led her back to her wagon. The next morning the woman walked over to Dever and Laura's wagon and talked to Dever in private, explaining what happened the night before. Dever was very concerned and could not let Laura out of his sight. Dever had to help out during the day and to man the wagon too. The next two weeks, everything went along as expected. The caravan had come to the first major river crossing. The wagon master told everyone to make sure everything was tied down and to stay together during the crossing.

"I don't want any wagons drifting downstream. The crossing will take some time, but we will move slowly across the river together." Dever and Laura's wagon was now in position. They were the next ones to enter the river.

"I want you to climb in the back and lie down until we are across," Dever told Laura.

"I don't want to climb in the back. I want to sit right here beside you," Laura replied.

"Suit yourself, but I believe it would be safer in the back of the wagon," Dever said. Dever had reached the river's edge, and the wagon wheels were now rolling into the water.

"Keep a tight hand on the reins and don't let the wagon head downstream," the wagon master shouted. They were now in the middle of the river, and the wagon began to roll because of the undercurrent.

"Hold on tight to the wagon cover!" Dever yelled to Laura.

Suddenly the wagon drifted into a hole and started to capsize. Laura was thrown from the wagon and was taken downstream by the rushing water. The man in the wagon behind them saw what was happening and yelled at Dever to hold on and that he would go after Laura. The man handed over the reins to his wife then jumped into the river and began swimming as fast as he could toward Laura, who was lying against the bank unconscious. The man made his way to Laura then pulled her upon the bank. Laura began to cough. She was all right and was just suffering from fatigue.

After reaching the other side of the river, everyone was accounted for. The wagon master decided to camp there for the night. Laura was now back in her wagon resting. This had become the worst day of the journey. Hunters would go out each day in search of meat for the passengers. The animal life was not abundant on the prairie; only a few antelopes could be found scattered around. For some reason the buffalo had migrated south about a hundred miles away from their normal grazing and water holes.

Laura had started to experience some minor labor pains. She was about seven months along. She had to carry the baby for another month or so if it was going to survive.

One stifling afternoon the wagon dropped into a deep rut in the middle of the trail, breaking off the wagon tongue. Dever stopped the team and got out to see what happened. The wagon tongue was broken into two pieces, leaving one end attached to the team and the other to the front of the wagon.

Dever yelled to the wagon master for help. After determining the problem, the wagon master said they would have find two pieces of wood to lash alongside of the broken tongue. Dever volunteered to search for some wood pieces to repair the wagon tongue. An hour later he came back with two long branches. The wagon master broke each of them in half into equal lengths. Two men held the wood pieces in place along the wagon tongue while holding the two broken pieces together. The wagon master soaked several pieces of rawhide and firmly wrapped them around the two wood pieces and the tongue.

"Hold these in place for about an hour, letting them shrink around the wagon tongue," the wagon master said.

The wagon tongue had been temporarily fixed, and everyone was ready to start moving out. The wagon train was somewhere in the Wyoming territory, and it was the end of August. Laura's contractions were growing closer together, but she still had about seven weeks to go full term. Late one night Laura woke screaming as loud as she could. She woke the entire encampment.

Dever jumped up and grabbed Laura, "What is wrong?" he yelled.

"I am going to have my baby, and I can't stand the pain," she replied.

Several women from the other wagons came running and were now at Laura's bedside. Laura was having painful contractions running about a minute apart. One of the women asked Dever to leave, telling him that she and the others would care for Laura and would keep him informed if anything happened.

"This is not a man's job. Please let us handle this," one of the women told Dever.

Dever left, not knowing what to expect. Within an hour one of the women came to Dever's side and told him he was a father of a baby girl, just like the one Laura had envisioned. Dever jumped up and ran to his wagon where he found Laura and his new daughter lying side by side. The baby looked healthy, but Laura did not look as well. She had been through an ordeal she never expected.

The days that followed were good. Laura and the baby were doing well. The following day, one of the scouts came back to the wagon train and reported that there was a cholera epidemic about five miles ahead; two wagons and ten people were camped there and were sick with the cholera.

They crossed and drank from the same river we crossed about five days before we did," the scout said, "I told them I would try to get back to them with some laudanum if we could spare any."

After hearing this, members of the wagon train were up in arms.

"What if we come down with cholera? We drank from the same water those people did!"

The wagon master stepped up on the side of a wagon and gathered everyone around.

"Listen, I don't want everyone to panic. There is no sign of cholera on this wagon train. This doesn't mean any of us have drunk contaminated water. Please calm down and go back to your wagons and hope for the best."

Two days later the wagon train caught up with the people suffering from cholera.

Two had died, and several of the others were still very sick but were showing some improvement.

The two who died were buried inside the wagon tracks to prevent marauding animals from digging up the remains and carrying them off across the prairie.

Help was given to the others with some of the more sick receiving doses of laudanum.

This was costing the wagon train serious time that could not be made up. Those continuing on bid farewell to those remaining and continued on.

"We just can't leave these sick people to die!" Laura shouted.

"There is nothing more we can do. We have no more time to spare here. It could be a matter of life or death for us on the other end!" the wagon master replied.

The following week Laura's baby began to cough and started with diarrhea.

Laura began to cry. "I don't want to lose my baby," she sobbed, "this is all I have to live for!"

Dever tried to comfort her. "What about me? Am I not a good reason to live for as well?" Dever asked.

"It's not the same, this baby means more to me than anything else in life," Laura replied.

"Our baby means as much to me as she does to you. She is our creation and is a marvelous gift from God. She is not yours or mine, she represents us both," Dever said.

Laura was not hearing a word that Dever had to say; she was somewhere else. That night the baby began to vomit along with the diarrhea. Laura woke up screaming. She grabbed the baby and began running from wagon to wagon, yelling at the top of her lungs, "My baby is dying! Please someone help me!" she yelled.

Dever jumped from the wagon, running up behind her. Dever tried to comfort Laura, but she was in a state of panic. Nothing he said or tried to do made any difference to Laura. Finally she fell to the ground in front of a horse tied to a wagon. She sat on the ground with the baby in her arms, rocking the infant and mumbling inaudibly. Dever kneeled down by her side. The baby was dead; the baby's skin had a grey cast with no sign of life.

Dever tried to take the baby from his wife's arms, but she wouldn't let the baby go. Laura was clinging on as to never let go. Everyone in the camp was now gathered around Laura and the baby. Laura just sat there rocking the baby. Dever sat down by Laura's side and waited for her to fall asleep. He took the baby from her arms and gently laid her on the ground, covering her with two heavy blankets. It was about two hours before sunup, and it was very chilly on the prairie. The wagon master and several of the women came to Dever's side.

"Here, let us help you with the baby," they said as they reached out and gave Dever a hug and took the baby from him. Laura was moved into the wagon where she could rest. Later that day Laura woke up.

"Where is my baby? Someone has stolen her!" she yelled out. One of the women came back holding Laura's baby wrapped in white linen. It had been prepared for burial.

"Laura, your baby is dead. We need to give her a proper service and burial, "The woman said.

"Give me my baby! She is not dead! You just want her for your own!" Laura screamed. Dever nodded for the woman to give Laura the baby.

Laura grabbed the baby from the woman's arms then held her close to her breasts.

"You all stay away from my baby, or she will die!" Laura shouted.

Dever tried to reason with her, but she was not listening to a word he said. Laura was delirious and living in her own world.

Dever decided to wait until Laura fell asleep; he would then take the baby out on the prairie and bury her. Several hours later, out of exhaustion, Laura fell asleep. The wagon master and two other people along with Dever buried the baby in the wagon tracks about two hundred yards behind them. There was no marker, just a stone off to the side indicating the baby's burial site and the date of death etched on it. After Laura had awakened, she immediately asked for her baby. Dever told Laura that he had buried the baby.

"Why did you bury her? She was not dead!" Laura said hysterically.

Dever turned to Laura and grabbed her by the shoulders. "Listen to me, the baby is dead, and there is nothing anyone can do to bring her back. You have to move on, or you will end up crazy," Dever said in a firm but loving voice.

Laura seemed to understand and said nothing more. Two days passed, and Dever began to smell something strange coming from the back of the wagon. Laura appeared to be back to her normal self, and everything was good again. The wagon train stopped for water, and Dever went through the back of the wagon. He found a small trunk that Laura had brought with her. He opened it up, and there were the remains of the baby. Laura had gone back during the night and dug up the baby and placed her tiny body in the trunk.

Dever told the wagon master what happened, and the wagon train was stopped long enough to explain to Laura that the baby had to be buried and left alone. The baby was dead, and nothing more could be done. One of the women had an idea and told Dever that several of the women had made a doll to give to Laura in place of the dead baby. Later that night the women brought the doll over and gave it to Laura. She accepted it as if they had brought her daughter back. Laura took the doll in her arms and drew it to her chest then murmured something. This was the greatest gift anyone could have given her. She had her baby back in her arms.

Sadly Laura never came out of her depression. Upon arriving in the Willamette Valley, Dever tried desperately over the next year to help Laura regain her health; however, he was ultimately left with no choice but to have Laura committed to an asylum. Laura lived out her remaining years before passing away of a broken heart in 1867.

HELL'S GATE

Major Jon Tremaine was the warden of Camp Douglas prison during the Civil War. The prison was located about eight hundred miles north of the enemy lines to house Confederate prisoners captured in the South. Major Tremaine was not only feared by the inmates but was also hated because of his merciless methods of discipline.

The rain was pouring down as two escapees were dragged back to the camp; the major looked on in his arrogant and sadistic way. It would be his decision to dish out the retribution for escaping. He stood above the prisoners standing on a wood-covered catwalk, looking down as if he were god himself and preparing for the next major event. The two men were laying in the mud which exposed their bruised and broken bodies, having been dragged over two miles back to the prison yard. The major always made an example of the runaways by having all the other prisoners watch the suffering of anyone defying his order of detention.

"Major, what should we do with these two?" one of the guards shouted.

"Stake them out on the ground and leave them for everyone to see!" The major shouted back.

"They could die. The ground is soaked, and they have little on to keep them warm," the other guard said.

"Just do as I have ordered, or you will be joining them," the major remarked in his normal defiant manner. The two men were staked out on the bare ground with their faces exposed to the choking rain. The men were coughing, trying to clear their throats while each shivered in the wet cold. The next morning the rain subsided, leaving one of the prisoners dead and the other suffering from hypothermia and pneumonia.

"Major, can we take the live one inside before he dies too?" the guard yelled.

"No, leave him out for a few more hours. If he survives then place him in solitary. Make sure you drag the other one outside the prison. This will give the animals something to eat on."

Later that day the rain stopped, and the prisoner lay unconscious on the ground shivering.

"Okay, boys, it looks like he's had enough. Place him in solitary confinement for a few days," the major quipped.

One morning, one of the guards approached the man placed in solitary confinement to give him food. There was no response; he had died during the night. The guard went down on his hands and knees and slowly pulled the dead man out of the hole. He was later buried outside the prison. The prisoners witnessing the harsh treatment began to protest the major's tactics by taking anything they had and pounding on the makeshift prison bars.

"If they don't shut up, throw the excrement from the trenches on them!" shouted the major.

Being threatened with excrement, the prisoners decided to calm down. Each day was the constant reminder of gruesome and inhumane treatment along with the cry of those dying everywhere. Some of the prisoners had been in the compound for over a year and had witnessed brothers and fathers succumbing to the hand of the major.

Following the severe rains winter found its way into the camp, leaving hundreds of men cold with little or nothing to eat. There were no outside provisions for the prisoners, only for the officers and enlisted men. As time went by it was determined that the lucky ones died on the battlefield, and the remainder ended up in the prison camp. Every few days, new captives were brought into the camp for indoctrination and terrible treatment. The major reveled in the hardship and suffering of the prisoners.

While the war continued, the months slowly passed with the addition and overcrowding of more and more prisoners. There were times when space to sleep became the focal point of the day, with fights breaking out among the prisoners. Several men were killed in these skirmishes. The other problem was lack of clothing and heat. Large fires were built in the middle of the prison yard, momentarily giving off heat for those gathered around. The flames quickly died, and so did the heat, leaving cold and unbearable conditions. The men's clothing was nothing more than rags that were torn, shredded, or were rotting away, with no means of replacing them.

The living conditions became so bad that dying men preferred to be left alone without treatment so that they may be allowed to die, setting them free from the untenable conditions of life. The only hope was that one day the war would end, and each man would be set free. The lack of food not only caused malnutrition but also delusionary thinking among certain prisoners. Not only were men dying because of hunger but also by killing each other because of ravaged minds that could no longer comprehend what was happening around them.

One day an ill-fated attempt on the major's life had failed. Twenty of the perpetrators were caught and tied to hitching posts inside the gathering area and were given fifty lashes each; then, they were left where they lie. Ten men were beaten to death with several others left in critical condition. The remainder slowly regained their health. One prisoner was left with a crippled left arm.

In early spring the major took ill and was moved from the prison to an outside facility.

With the major gone a group of men decided to overpower the guards and break out. After leaving the camp the men followed the lake for five miles looking for a way to cross. They were tired and hungry, and they needed to rest. By now the prison guards were close behind. The sound of bloodhounds could be heard in the distance. Somehow, they need to find a way across the lake, or the dogs would overtake them. Two hours later the blood hounds had caught up with them and had the men cornered in a thicket near the lake bank. There was no way out. The guards escorted then back to the prison where they were placed in solitary confinement until a decision could be made about their fate. Ironically, the major had gotten better; he returned to the camp to assume his previous position. Inside the prison, a large flag pole with a yardarm attached—once a part of an English sailing ship—became a focal point for making examples of the worst men. This was used not only for the prisoners but also for insubordinate union army enlistees as well.

Following two weeks in solitary confinement the major ordered every man involved brought forth to hear the charges and sentencing. Of the twenty, only sixteen were still alive. The major read each name and found each of them guilty of killing two guards and fleeing the camp as escaped prisoners during time of war.

"I find each of you guilty on all accounts and sentence each of you to hang off the yardarm until you're dead. The sentencing will be carried out at sunup tomorrow," the major said in a stern voice.

The prisoners yelled out in great protest. "You just can't hang everyone for trying to escape!" the men shouted. The major ignored them by turning away and walking back inside his quarters.

The following morning three empty wagons were brought in lined up behind those being hanged. Each prisoner had a blindfold placed over his head while standing on a whiskey barrel waiting for the major's nod before kicking the barrel out from beneath each of the prisoners, one at a time. The major wanted everyone to witness the horrific scene over and over, so it would be etched in each prisoner's mind. Following the last execution the bodies were loaded in the wagons; they were taken outside the prison to be buried in a mass grave about two hundred yards east of the main entrance to a wooded area.

The prisoners were thrown into a fit of rage trying to deal with a madman. In the process of the barbarism a deep alliance was formed among most of the prisoners.

One man stood out as a natural leader and had gained the trust of everyone inside the prison. Arch Pierce was always there to calm the fears of the men and quell attempts of rioting and killing of the guards. It was agreed that when the war was over they would seek retribution against the major. No man alive could live with the images of persecution and needless death that each had witnessed at the major's hand without seeking relief of his own soul. Fortunately, this would be the last winter before the war ended.

It was April 1865, and the war had officially ended. It took several weeks before word reached the outside world, including the prison called Hell's Gate. On the morning of May 20, 1865, the major, standing aloof on his catwalk perch above everyone, summoned all the guards, ordering that all the prisoners be set free as the war was over. The large gates leading outside the compound were opened, followed by a mass exodus. After much celebration and shouting, some of the prisoners did not know where to go. Some were disoriented while others suffered mental and physical problems. Many of the men would perish en route back home. Some had to travel several hundred miles to reach their families and farms. The process of repatriation would take several months.

In the spring of 1866, Arch Pierce determined it was time to assemble all those still alive and willing to pursue retribution against Major Jon Tremaine for all the atrocities and murdering of innocent prisoners while under his command. The first thing Arch did was send out telegrams to every town that had a telegraph office in the Southern states, requesting anyone available to meet on August 20 outside Springfield, Missouri. The day before, Arch rode into town to look for suitable space for the men to camp. To the north was an open area that had been used as a supply center and had been abandoned. This appeared to be a good place to build a camp.

The following day and a week later, men from all over converged on the little town looking for Arch Pierce. After everyone was in the camp, Arch discussed his plan to find the major and to hand out proper punishment for what would be considered war crimes while being detained by the enemy.

"I want ten volunteers to ride north with me tomorrow in search of Major Jon Tremaine's farm. The rest of you are to remain here until we return. This should take only two to three days," Arch told everyone. Prior to the men's arrival, he had supplied the camp with food paid for by himself. This was not to be another ill-fated plan. Driven by the courage of one man, the men left with only clothing on their backs and minimal rations, not knowing how long they would be gone.

Several of the men shouted, "What if you don't come back?"

"We will be back, but if something happens and we don't, all of you should return to your homes," Arch shouted.

The following day Arch and the others arrived at Naperville, Illinois. Arch inquired about the major, telling the local townspeople he was an old friend and just wanted to look him up if he lived in the area.

"You know, mister, the last I heard the major had bought a place outside Chicago. I don't know for sure though," the old man said.

"Much obliged, mister," Arch replied. Arch and the others continued on toward Chicago. They camped along a roadway and decided to scout out the area the next day. Arch left the others behind and told them he would be back by nightfall. Arch was riding toward Chicago when he came upon a man carrying supplies in a wagon headed south.

"Pardon me, sir. I was wondering if you could help me. I am looking for Major Jon Tremaine's place. We are old friends, and I have not seen him since the war," Arch asked.

"Mister, you are on the right road. Just keep headed north until you come to Donner's Grove. The major's place is about two miles east. You can't miss it. You will see a large red barn on the right. That is the beginning of the major's spread."

"Thanks, mister."

Arch turned his horse around and headed back to meet the others waiting for him. Back in camp he sent three riders back to Naperville to bring everyone to the campsite. The next day Arch summoned everyone around to give them instructions for the next day.

"I want everyone to surround the major's farm. We should be there by sunset tomorrow. I don't want any fires or loud noises. We don't want to alarm him or his family."

By the end of the next day everyone was bedded down around the major's farm waiting for sunup. Arch gave the signal for everyone to rise and to slowly close in on the farm. Arch along with two others walked up the long path leading to the white-pillared farmhouse. Arch knocked on the door. A woman greeted him, asking if she could help.

"Yes, ma'am, I am looking for the major. Is he hereabout?" Arch asked.

"Please wait here, and I will see if he is available," the woman replied. A few minutes later the major came to the door then walked out on the large front porch.

"How may I help you, sir?" he said before looking up.

Suddenly the major realized who was standing in front of him and started to draw his gun.

Before anything happened, Arch and the other men had their pistols drawn, pointing directly at the major's head.

"Now, Major, I am sure you remember me and some of the others, don't you?" Arch said as he motioned for everyone surrounding the farm to come closer. "Take his pistol."

The two men removed the major's pistol then backed him up against the wall.

"What are you doing here? What are you going to do with me?" the major asked as he swallowed his voice.

"In case you need your memory refreshed, I am going to tell you why we are here. Did you really believe you could treat us and all the others who didn't make it while in your prison like a bunch of common criminals or rejects from society, then become the sole judge, jury, and executioner, without any for thought or mercy because of our incarceration in your prison? Mister, in case you don't know, you are not God Almighty. You are nothing more than a man like we are but are far less fortunate at this moment in time." By now the major's family was standing on the porch by his side.

"Take the major's wife and three children over there," he pointed toward the end of the porch, "while I read the charges against this less than a man before everyone," Arch said in a matter-of-fact voice. Arch began to read the full account of the charges against the major, listing each of them in chronological order. This process lasted over one hour. Arch turned to the major's wife and children and said, "No family should live in the shadow of a man who possesses no humility or shame but was empowered to command death and destruction on others because of his position in life. I want you to take the major back to the barn and tie him up inside to one of the crossbeams," Arch directed.

Several men dragged the major to the barn while he was kicking and screaming, "This isn't right! You can't do this to me!" he yelled.

"You gave up your rights a long time ago, and now you must pay for your crimes," Arch replied. After lashing the major to a beam everyone left the barn. The major's wife was screaming, and she started toward the barn.

"Someone grab her!" Arch yelled, then he motioned for several of the men to pour coal oil around the base of the barn and light it.

The major's wife and children had to be restrained.

The fire was lit, and the barn soon began to burn. After a few minutes Arch decided to enter the barn and bring the major outside if he was still alive. Arch threw a watered-down blanket over his body then entered the barn. He found the major unconscious, lying on the ground. He quickly grabbed him by the legs and dragged him outside.

The major was barely alive, but his face was burned beyond recognition. Arch motioned for his men to release the major's wife and children before riding away.

I AM MY BROTHER'S KEEPER

It was August of 1845, and Tandey Hawthorne was one of many slaves working on the Hawthorne plantation. Tandey had been a slave since his birth and had worked the fields since he was eight years old. Tandey worked alongside his father, mother, and younger sister for as long as he could remember. Tandey had yearned for a better life but had never experience the outside world, only through the stories of the whites. Tandey was intrigued by what lay beyond the plantation walls that kept him and the others in. Today Tandey was dreaming of what life might be like living off the plantation.

"Tandey, get back to work, there is much to be done before nightfall!" one of the white overseers shouted.

"Yes, sir, I am sorry, sir. It won't happen again," Tandey replied.

"You know what we do with lazy niggers, we whip the hell out of them!" the overseer yelled. Tandey had been beaten on a regular basis for as long as he was old enough to remember. Today he decided to escape this horrible way of life or be killed.

A close friend tried escape a year before but was caught and brought back to the plantation and taken to the woodshed. The overseer laid his left foot on a large log then chopped his left foot with a double-sided ax. The young man screamed at the loss of his foot and just about died from loss of blood and from shock.

The overseer shouted in his face, "Now try running away nigger!"

Two family members wrapped what was left of the young man's foot in a piece of muslin; they took him back to a nearby shack where they cauterized his foot with a searing hot knife blade before bandaging him up.

Either way, it did not matter—Tandey knew this was no way to live! The sun began to set on the fields, and the last ray of light shone against the endless rows of cotton. Just before the sun set Tandey lied down between the rows of waiting until everyone had left the field. After everyone was gone he crawled on his hands and knees to the far end of the field, then he slowly climbed over the stone wall before dropping to the ground on the other side. Tandey knew it would not be long before they realized he was missing and would send out the bloodhounds to track him down. If he could get far enough before sunup he might have a chance to escape. The plantation owner would not try to track him at night.

Tandey ran as fast as he could in the moonlight toward a small stream.

The stream ran north and south, so he decided to enter the water and walk as far as possible before leaving the stream. It would be more difficult for the blood hounds to pick up his scent.

Morning came, and Tandey was suffering from fatigue. He needed food and rest, but he knew the men and dogs were still after him; there's no way of telling what would happen if they caught up with him. Tandey could be strung up by the neck at the nearest tree rather than be taken back. There was no choice but to keep on moving north, as far away from the plantation as possible.

The following day Tandey came upon a small farmhouse and barns situated in the middle of a field. Tandey circled around behind the barn and waited until dark, then he moved inside and quickly fell asleep on the hay. Early before dawn Tandey left the barn and continued north. There was no trace of the bloodhounds or the men following him. About a week later he arrived in the New Mexico territory. Tandey followed the waterways, foraging for food along the way.

Three weeks passed, and Tandey was weakened because of the lack of food; he had stumbled into a small Mescalero Apache settlement before collapsing of exhaustion. A woman saw him lying in the grass and yelled for help. Four braves ran to where the woman stood. The entire village stood around, gaping at Tandey; none had ever seen a black man before. The braves picked Tandey up and carried him into a teepee.

A woman inside by the name of Preyasi ("beloved") agreed to care for Tandey. Preyasi had never seen a black man and was curious about him and where he was from. One morning Tandey was awakened by Preyasi lying next to him, comparing skin colors by placing her hand on his.

Tandey spoke only English and had never had any conversations with Indians, especially having lived in the South. He tried his best to understand the Apache and to explain that he had been a slave since birth like his father and mother. Tandey asked permission to stay in the camp for a few days to regain his strength before moving on. At first he was not welcome, but after a couple of days, everyone seemed to adjust to the black stranger and his odd ways of speaking and eating. Preyasi was growing fond of Tandey, and she did not want him to leave. She would sit by him each day and rub his face. He had a rough beard and short wiry hair, which Preyasi had never seen before. This man was different from any other men she had been around. Each morning Preyasi would walk with Tandey, trying to communicate the best she could. Tandey was growing stronger, and he knew it was time for him to leave.

Preyasi realized it was time for Tandey to leave.

She reached out, taking Tandey by the hand; she looked into his eyes and told him in Apache that she did not want him to leave and that she was falling in love with him.

Though Preyasi's words were not directly understood, Tandey knew what she was saying. He felt the same way too. Preyasi had a special sweetness about her that made Tandey want to be with her always. As time went by Tandey began to understand and speak a few words in Apache. Preyasi tried hard to understand Tandey and was able to repeat some of his words well. The process was slow, but each of them was learning how to communicate more easily.

After learning more about Tandey and his past, the tribe was willing to let him stay and continue his relationship with Preyasi. Preyasi was regarded as a trusted and valued member of the tribe. Tandey wanted to ask her to marry him but decided, out of respect, he would talk to the chief and ask his permission first. The chief was well pleased and honored that Tandey would ask his permission to marry Preyasi. The chief readily approved but did show some concern about two people from different cultures and races raising a family together.

"I understand your concerns, and I respect both yours and Preyasi's culture," Tandey replied.

"Then go forth, my son, and become one spirit with Preyasi and live as a man and wife in your own lodge together."

After receiving the chief's permission Tandey asked Preyasi for her hand in marriage which she readily accepted. Both Tandey and Preyasi decided to move away from her people and begin fresh by building a farm of their own outside of the small village of Tularosa.

Tandey filed the necessary paperwork for a homestead. He and Preyasi received one hundred and sixty acres to improve and eventually own, provided he and Preyasi live on and improve the property for a continuous five years, after which they would receive a free and clear deed to the property. With the help of Preyasi's people a small but livable adobe cabin was built. Later on Tandey built a barn to the rear of the small cabin. Time passed, and the farm flourished, and two sons were born to Preyasi and Tandey. Years later the two boys turned into fine men and decided to go in separate ways. The oldest boy was Hemmet, and he wanted to become a lawman; the other, Kagan, wanted to become a rancher. Before the two boys left the ranch, Preyasi said she had something for each of them.

"Come here, my sons. I want you to have these to remember me by," Preyasi said. She handed each of them a headstall for their horses. One was made of black leather and was decorated with horn, beads, and horsehair. The other was brown leather, decorated in the same manner. They were to be used as part of the bridle.

The two sons each gave their mother a kiss and thanked her for her love.

"We will always remember you, Mother. You have always shown your love to us over the years. We will miss you and Father too."

The next three years brought much change. Preyasi became ill with smallpox, and she died. Tandey struggled to work the homestead with the help of two other men, but life was never the same following the death of Preyasi.

Kagan had since married a Mexican woman from Santa Fe, and together they raised three daughters. Kagan decided to move back to his father's farm to help him.

"I don't need your help, and besides, you have your own family to raise," Tandey told him.

"But Father, you do need my help. The place is becoming rundown, and it needs much work. The other problem is that you can't trust the two men working for you. I will sell my small spread and move down here with you, Father." After much discussion Tandey reluctantly agreed to let Kagan and his family move back to his spread.

Hemmet had moved to the Wyoming territory where he took a job as a deputy sheriff in the small town of Pinedale. The sheriff was a man of large stature and a commanding voice. He had political aspirations of running for territorial governor, but he needed someone who could step up and take over as sheriff. Hemmet was a good lawman but could not be bribed. He was straightforward and honest.

Hemmet married a young woman named Dodie Stephens; she worked as a dancehall girl. He fell in love with her when he first came to town. They had been married for about six months when he accepted the job as deputy sheriff.

A wealthy landowner, Matt Jacobs, owned most of the town and a large spread outside as well. He was well connected politically, and he bought off or killed anyone in his path. The sheriff had been on Matt's payroll since he took office. He was paid to look the other way if something involving Matt or his men came up. Hemmet could not be bought off. Matt had threatened him several times for throwing some of his men in jail for causing trouble or breaking the peace while liquored up. The sheriff told Hemmet to take some time off and go fishing or go back home for a few days to clear his head and get away.

I'll see you are paid, so don't worry about paying your bills," the sheriff told him.

"You can't buy me because I have been upholding the law when it comes to Matt's men who break the law every time they come to town," Hemmet said.

"It is for your own good, Hemmet. I wouldn't want to see anything happen to you, that's all," the sheriff said.

"I'm not worried about Matt Jacobs or his men. I am just trying to do my job."

"You know, Hemmet, I am going to be campaigning for governor next year, and I need someone like you to take over. You have done an excellent job, but there is one thing you need to remember. You have to get along with Matt Jacobs."

"What you are telling me, Sheriff, is that Matt Jacobs owns this town and everyone here, including you. He may be able to buy you off or some of the others, but I am not going along with his tactics," Hemmet replied.

"Well, Hemmet, if anything happens, you can't say I didn't warn you," the sheriff said.

"What could happen? Is Matt going to kill me if I don't do everything his way?"

"All I'm saying, Hemmet, you are walking a fine line. I would hate to see anything happen to you or your pretty wife."

"You know, Sheriff, if you don't think I'm good enough to fill your shoes by doing what's right, then maybe we should part company," Hemmet said in a firm voice.

"Now don't get all worked up. Just try taking things a little easier, and everything will be just fine," the sheriff replied. Hemmet knew from that moment on that the sheriff was on the take and would do whatever Matt Jacobs asked him to do. Hemmet never discussed his job with Dodie.

One Saturday night, three of Matt's men got involved in a drunken brawl at the Roadway Saloon. Hemmet went over to break up the fight. Hemmet drew his gun, "You three men are under arrest," he said as he pointed his gun toward the men. Suddenly a man from behind struck Hemmet in the head with a whiskey bottle, knocking him to the floor. The three men laughed while they dragged Hemmet out into the street and left him there. Blood was running down his face; his head was cut open, leaving a two-inch gash. Hemmet lied unconscious until two men coming out of the saloon saw him there. They picked him up and took him across the street to Doc Bennigan's office. It was about midnight when one of the men knocked on the office door.

"What do you want? Don't you know what time it is?" the doc shouted.

"We have a man out here. He's been hurt, come on and open up!" one of the men yelled.

"Okay, just a minute, let me get my pants on." The doc opened the door and said, "Lay him over there," as he pointed to a large wooden table with a sheet covering it.

"You men go ahead and clear out so, I can do my job. I'll let you know how he is when I am done, now move." Hemmet had a large gash on the back of his head where the whiskey bottle landed.

The doc stitched him up and made him lie still for a while.

"Hemmet, who did this to you?"

"It must have been one of Matt Jacobs's men. I went into the saloon to break up a fight, and the next thing I knew, I was hit from behind. I don't remember anything after that."

"You need to lie here and take it easy for a couple of hours. You have had a concussion too, "The doc said. The doc went outside and told the other men Hemmet would be all right; he just needed some rest. Later that day Hemmet left the doctor's office and staggered across the street where he and his wife were staying. Hemmet lay down waiting for Dodie to come home.

That night he told her what happened, and Dodie began to cry. "I don't want anything to happen to you. Maybe we should move to another town."

"I don't want you to worry. Everything will be all right. I just need to ride out and have a chat with Matt Jacobs. I think I can get this whole situation straightened out."

"I don't think that is a good idea! I beg of you not to go. They could kill you, and no one would ever know what happened," Dodie said.

"I am sorry, but I need to get control of this situation before anything else happens."

The next day Hemmet rode out to talk to Matt Jacobs about his men coming to town and causing trouble. Hemmet rode through the large gate bearing the Lazy M brand leading to the large log home. Hemmet climbed down from his horse and knocked on the front door.

Right away an elderly Mexican woman greeted him and asked, "How may I help you?"

"My name is Hemmet, and I am here to see Mr. Jacobs," Hemmet said.

"Please come inside, and I will see if Mr. Jacobs will see you."

Matt entered the room and asked, "Hemmet, I meant to drop by and tell you how sorry I am for what one of my men did to you. I want to make it up to you, so I want to give you a hundred dollars to pay the medical bills and something a little extra for you and your wife."

"Don't patronize me. I didn't come here for a handout. You keep your money. I just want your men to control their drinking and fighting when they come to town. Every Saturday night it is the same problem."

"I understand and I will talk to my men and make sure these problems don't happen again," Matt assured him.

"I'll be on my way then," Hemmet said as he walked out the door.

After Hemmet had left the house Matt summoned for two of his men to follow and make sure he didn't get back to town. "One thing, though. Whatever happens it needs to look like an accident. Do you understand?" Matt shouted.

"Yes, boss," the two men replied.

The two men followed Hemmet, riding in the shadows; they finally caught up with him, riding on each side then kicked him off his horse. Hemmet went to pull his gun, but one of the men knocked it out of his hand using a rifle butt. Both men wrestled Hemmet to the ground while one tied his hands behind him and the other his feet. "We're going to show you what we do with troublemakers." One of the men threw a rope over a low hanging tree branch of an old Cottonwood tree, and the other end was tied around Hemmet's neck.

Hemmet yelled, "Why are you doing this?"

"Let's say for Matt Jacobs's benefit." The loose end of the rope was tied to one of the men's saddle horn, pulling Hemmet off the ground. The man rode to the trunk of the tree then walked his horse around it until the rope was firmly wrapped, leaving Hemmet screaming and gasping for breath while slowly choking to death at the same time. In a matter of seconds Hemmet's body went limp.

"Well, that should take care of that," one of the men said as they rode back to the ranch. No sooner had the two men ridden out of sight than the old tree branch snapped crashing to the ground, taking Hemmet with it.

Both riders went back to the main house and told Matt what they did. Matt told them he would handle everything from here on out.

Hemmet's horse made its way back to town and wandered over in front of the sheriff's office and just stood there, as if he was waiting for someone. Everyone on the street looked at the horse, wondering where Hemmet was. The sheriff came out and asked everyone to go home; he would look for Hemmet and find out what happened right away.

Hemmet lay motionless on the ground with the rope still taut around his neck. He began gasping for air and realized he was not dead. He slowly removed the noose from around his neck by reaching with both hands—which were still tied together—and pulling it over his head. He reached down and untied his legs before working both hands loose. Hemmet's neck had been severely burned by the rope. He slowly got up and decided to walk to town. He knew if Matt Jacobs and his men found him alive, they would kill him and Dodie.

Hemmet decided to wait for nightfall before returning to town. After walking for nearly two hours in the shadows along the roadway, he made his way to town; staying out of the light, he circled around to the backstreet then entered his room. He walked in the door and heard a scream. It was Dodie; she thought someone was breaking in. She soon realized it was Hemmet and that he was in a bad way. Before a word was spoken, Hemmet fell on the floor, passed out.

Dodie ran to his side and bent over him; she was afraid he was dead. She laid her head on his chest, and she could hear his heart beating. Dodie kneeled down on the floor, patiently holding Hemmet's head in her lap and waiting for him to wake up. Two hours later, Hemmet began to show signs of life again. He told Dodie what happened and that they had to get out of town as soon as possible; otherwise, they would be hunted down like two wild animals and would be shot on sight. Matt Jacobs and his men are killers and will stop at nothing to protect their spoils.

Hemmet asked, "Have you seen my horse?"

"No, I haven't. I thought he might come back to town, especially after what happened."

"It really doesn't matter. We need to get out of here now! When we come back, the law will be with us," Hemmet told Dodie.

"Where will we go?" Dodie asked.

"We will go to Rock Springs, where they have a United States Marshal. It will take us about three days of hard riding. I'm going to the livery stable and bring your horse back and tie him up in back. I will try to find or buy another horse. Pack light for both of us so we can leave when I return."

"Are sure you are able to ride tonight?" Dodie asked.

"We don't have a choice. Just be ready when I get back."

The street was dark as Hemmet ran down the boardwalk. After reaching the livery stable, the door was locked.

He pounded on the door until Earl Gibbons, the owner, came to the doors and shouted, "Who is it?"

"It's Hemmet. Please open up."

"Do you know what time it is anyway? Can't you wait until morning?"

"Matter of fact I can't. Dodie and I are leaving for Riverton. Her father has taken ill and isn't expected to live," Hemmet replied.

"The sheriff came by earlier and said your horse came back without you, and that he was going out in the morning and look for you. The strange thing though, he didn't seem too upset. What happened anyway?"

"Oh, I was riding when my horse stumbled in a prairie dog hole and threw me. I walked back to town with just a lump on my head. Earl, please don't mention I was here tonight, will you?"

"Well, okay, if you insist!"

"I noticed my horse is in the back of the stable with Dodie's. The sheriff must have brought him over? Can you help me saddle up, so I can get going?"

The two horses were saddled, and Hemmet rode over to where he and Dodie were staying. Dodie had everything ready. After tying on the bedrolls and other supplies they left town, headed for Rock Springs. Hemmet told Dodie what he said to Earl at the livery stable, hoping to throw everyone off after they started looking for him and Dodie.

"I don't know how much time we have, but we need to ride the rest of the night to get as far away from here as we can. It won't take them very long to figure things out. We might have a day but not more."

By sunup Hemmet and Dodie were well on their way out of town.

The sheriff had ridden out to Matt Jacobs's place looking for Hemmet when he was greeted by Matt and two of his men.

"What are you doing here Sheriff," Matt asked?

"I came out looking for Hemmet. I know he rode out here yesterday, but his horse was the only thing that came back."

"Don't worry about Hemmet. He's all right," Matt said.

"What do you mean? Where is he?" the sheriff asked.

"Didn't you notice him hanging from a tree as you were riding this way?"

"No, I didn't see anything. Just a broken tree branch near the road, that's all," the sheriff replied.

Matt turned to his men and asked, "I thought you two had taken care of everything, that Hemmet was dead?"

The four men together went back along the road looking for Hemmet.

"Over here, this is the tree branch we hanged Hemmet on," one of the men shouted.

"I don't see any sign of Hemmet!" Matt yelled. "A dead man just doesn't walk off! Are you two stupid, or do we have a bigger problem?"

There was no sign of Hemmet, just a broken tree branch.

"Why did you want to kill Hemmet?" the sheriff asked.

Matt told him that Hemmet had been out to see him about his men causing trouble in town and that he was just getting in the way of progress.

"Sheriff, it is up to you to find Hemmet and bring him to me!" Matt shouted.

"This is going too far. This is where I draw the line. I don't want any part of any killings!" the sheriff remarked.

"Sheriff, you are right. You don't have to do anything at all," Matt said as he drew his gun and shot him. The sheriff fell to the ground.

"You two idiots get him out of here and meet me back in town." Matt left for town at a full gallop. He pulled up in front of the livery stable and jumped off his horse.

"Earl, have you seen Hemmet?"

"Why, no, I haven't. Is there a problem?"

"If you haven't seen him, then where are he and his wife's horses? You better not be lying to me, or you'll be a dead man very soon."

In a scared voice Earl said, "He did tell me that he and his wife were headed for Riverton and that her father was ill, and they needed to get there as soon as they could."

"Is that all?" Matt shouted as he grabbed Earl by the collar of his shirt.

"Yes, sir, that's all Hemmet told me."

"You'd better be right. Your life depends on it!" Matt shouted.

Matt's men from the ranch and the townspeople were out in the street.

"Everyone, go back to where you came from. This doesn't concern you!" Matt shouted. "I want you," he said as he pointed toward Merle and six men, "to take the road to Riverton. Stretch, you take the others and head toward Rock Springs. There is no time to waste. We can't take any chances. Whoever brings Hemmet and his wife back will receive two hundred dollars each. Now don't disappoint me!"

The townspeople didn't know what to do but to just stay away from Matt Jacobs and his men; they were ruthless and would stop at nothing.

Hemmet and Dodie had ridden the remainder of the first night and all day. They were a little more than a day from Rock Springs. Hemmet knew Matt's men would be riding as hard as they could to find him and Dodie. If they caught up with them they would either be killed on sight or be taken back to Pinedale. It didn't matter; either way, they would end up dead.

That afternoon it started to rain, slowing Hemmet and Dodie down. They were riding into a headwind driving the rain into their faces. They would have to stop and hope the rain let up. Hemmet led Dodie under a rock overhang out of the rain. They climbed down from their horses and waited for the weather to break. About an hour later the rain stopped, and they mounted up and continued on. The sky clouded over again, and nightfall set in.

They would have to stop; it was starting to rain again. The lightning and clap of thunder scared the horses. Hemmet hobbled them, so they couldn't run away. Early the following morning they packed up and continued on. They had lost so much time; they had no way of knowing how far behind them Matt's men were. They would ride as long as it took to reach Rock Springs; otherwise, their lives would be in jeopardy until then.

Dodie began to cry. "I am afraid they will catch up with us and kill us," she said.

"Don't be afraid. I won't let anything happen to you, I promise."

Following a long day and night of riding they finally arrived in Rock Springs. Hemmet and Dodie rode through the town looking for the marshal's office. There it was on the right side of the street.

They stopped in front and tied their horses up.

"Stay here with the horses. I will try to find someone," Hemmet said.

There were no lights on inside. Hemmet walked up to the front door and knocked several times. A few minutes later Hemmet heard the door unlock.

"Who is it, and do you have any idea what time it is, mister?" the marshal shouted.

"Yes, Sheriff, I do. This is a matter of life or death!" Hemmet shouted.

The sheriff opened the door and asked Hemmet and Dodie to come inside. Hemmet explained who he was and what had happened.

"How do I know you're telling the truth?" the marshal asked. Hemmet removed the scarf around his neck, exposing the terrible rope burns and laceration where he was hanged.

"Do you think I made this up, Marshal?"

"I am sorry, son. Now I understand your concerns," the marshal replied apologetically. "By the way, my name is Streck Hagan," the marshal said as he extended his hand to Hemmet.

Hemmet reached out and shook the marshal's hand and said, "I'm Hemmet Hawthorne, the deputy sheriff from Pinedale, and this is my wife Dodie." Hemmet had the marshal's interest, and he was ready to go something about the matter.

"Somehow, we must have gotten here ahead Matt Jacobs's men to town. Of course they could have turned back by now and returned to Pinedale," Hemmet said.

"How many of the townspeople are on Matt Jacobs's payroll?" the marshal asked.

"I don't know for sure, but I'm guessing at least forty or more," Hemmet replied.

"It's going to take a large posse to clean up the town. I will need help," the marshal said.

"I plan on helping you, Marshal, and I plan to have my brother come also. He lives in New Mexico, but he is good with a gun," Hemmet said. Hemmet turned to Dodie and said, "You need to go to New Mexico and stay with my father until this whole mess is over. The next stage leaves tomorrow at 8:00 a.m. I want you to be on it. It is just too dangerous to have you here."

The marshal sent a telegram to the sheriff in Riverton asking for his help. The next day an answer came back. The sheriff wanted to know more about the situation in Pinedale and how many men he should bring. At the same time Hemmet sent a telegram to his brother, Kagan, telling him that he was sending his wife Dodie to New Mexico where she would be safe.

Hemmet asked Kagan to leave as soon as possible, that he desperately needed his help and that he would explain later.

The marshal's plan was to have everyone together in five days to go over the plan to clean up Pinedale. The following week Kagan arrived in Rock Springs, and Dodie had made it safely to New Mexico.

After all the recruiting, there were about sixty men ready to help clean up Pinedale. The marshal had contacted the commander at Fort Laramie and asked for his help if needed. Captain Phillip Sebastian was a longtime friend, and he agreed to send a detachment if marshal law had to be invoked.

The marshal's plan was to divide then men into four groups and eventually surround the town. It would take about four days to have everyone in place before moving in. Once the marshal and his men were close to town, he would fire two shots to let everyone know he and his men were in position.

"I want to ride in first with my men and see if we can handle this peaceably first," the marshal told everyone.

The day had come, and the marshal led his men down the main street of Pinedale. The townspeople looked on with fear on each of their faces. Was this a gang of killers coming to take over the town? No one knew! The marshal moved slowly down the street before stopping in front of the sheriff's office. He climbed down from his horse and opened the door. There was no one inside.

"Where is the sheriff?" he asked.

One man spoke up, "The sheriff is gone. No one has seen him for a couple of weeks."

"What do you mean gone? Is he somewhere around, or is he dead?" the marshal asked.

"We honestly don't know," some of the townspeople replied.

"This seems might strange to me. The sheriff just disappears, and no one knows where he is. Let me ask you another question. Where can I find Matt Jacobs?"

"Mr. Jacobs must be at his ranch," one of the men said as he pointed to the northwest. "His spread is about five miles from here. You may want to be careful. He keeps everything under heavy guard!"

Some of the men had come out of the bars and stood in the street. One of them shouted, "Who do you think you are? Riding into our town and scaring the hell out of everyone!"

"Mister, I'll tell you who I am and why we are here! My name is Streck Hagan. I am a United States Marshal from Rock Springs, and we are here to get to the bottom of the killings that has been going on here for too long."

"Mr. Jacobs is not going to take kindly to your coming here. This is his town and everything around it," the cowboy stated.

"Frankly, cowboy, that's not our concern. We are not here to make friends but to clean this mess up!"

At that moment, the man talking and two other men drew their guns and started shooting, killing two of the marshal's men. Kagan and Hemmet drew their guns and shot all three standing in the street. The marshal yelled for everyone not to panic. Several other men came out of the some of the other buildings, shooting their way out of town. The shots were heard by the others waiting outside of town. They knew something was wrong as there were more than two shots fired.

As the others started for town to help the marshal, the men trying to escape ran into the other men who were coming in to help; they were immediately arrested. The town was completely encircled by the four groups of men, allowing no one to leave. Hemmet and Kagan ran out of town and toward Matt Jacobs's ranch. There was one more debt to be settled. They knew Matt would be waiting for them. So they waited until dark to move in. There were four men in front guarding the ranch. Hemmet knew there were others inside protecting Matt.

Hemmet motioned for Kagan to circle around the end of the house while he went back the other way to the barn.

Hemmet said, "I don't want to take any chances, so I am going to set the barn on fire. When they come out of the house you take the ones on the left, and I will take the ones on the right.

"Okay, brother," Kagan said.

Hemmet moved cautiously toward the barn, staying in the shadows. He slowly opened the door and pulled down a kerosene lantern, spilling the kerosene over the hay. He pulled out a match and lit it. Before the blaze started Hemmet moved away from the barn. Within minutes the barn ignited and started to burn.

One of the men standing on the porch yelled, "Help! There's a fire in the barn!" He and several other men headed toward the barn when Hemmet stepped out and drew his gun, killing one of them. By now Matt and the others in the house had come outside. After they cleared the doorway, Kagan began shooting. One of the men shot him in the arm while Matt Jacobs ran toward his horse in front of the house. Hemmet turned just in time to see Matt trying to mount his horse. His horse was scared and was turning in a circle because of the flames. Hemmet yelled for Matt to turnaround. Matt slapped his horse then fired at Hemmet, hitting him in his left leg.

Hemmet fell to the ground as Matt approached him with gun in hand.

Matt bent over and said, "Well, I figured this would end this way," when a shot rang out.

Kagan had shot Matt in the back; Matt fell on Hemmet. Matt was dead. Hemmet and Kagan slowly mounted up and rode back to Pinedale where the marshal and the others had rounded up the last of Matt Jacobs's men.

It was over; Kagan and Hemmet left and rode back to New Mexico. Shortly after Hemmet returned to New Mexico, he received a telegram asking him to come back to Pinedale and become the sheriff. Hemmet accepted, and he and Dodie returned to Wyoming where they lived out their lives in peace.

INCIDENT ON THE SNAKE RIVER

It had been two days since leaving the Circle R Ranch. John Crow had stopped at the Circle R to buy a fresh horse. His horse had gone lame about five miles before he reached the ranch. The Circle R was a large operation owned by a man named Judd Raker. Judd's ranch spanned over sixty thousand acres. He employed over a hundred ranch hands to run the day-to-day cattle operation. Judd also rounded up mustangs and broke them in when he needed fresh horse. He had a heart as big as his ranch; however, if anyone ever crossed him he would pay the price.

John rode up to the main ranch house and had just stepped down from his horse when he heard a man ask, "What can I do for you, cowboy?" John looked up and saw a large man standing on the front porch.

"Well sir, my horse went lame about five miles back, and I desperately need another one," John replied.

"Come on up here and sit a spell. You look like you're beat. By the way, my name is Judd Raker. I own this spread."

John reached out to shake Judd's hand and replied, "I am John Crow. Nice to meet you."

"Why don't you come inside, and I'll have Sadie whip up something to eat?"

"Mr. Raker, I don't want to impose on your hospitality. Really, all I need is a horse."

"Don't worry, John, we'll take care of the horse after you've had some of Sadie's home cookin'."

Judd opened the large front door leading down the hallway to the kitchen.

"Just sit wherever you want, John. Sadie will have some food out shortly," Judd said. After John had eaten, he and Judd went out to one of the corrals to look over the horse.

"Well, son, just pick out whichever one you want, and then we'll settle up," Judd said.

"Mr. Raker, I don't have much money. I can only pay about twenty dollars, if that will buy anything?"

"That sounds fine with me, son. Just let me know which one you want, and we have a deal. And by the way, if ever you get back to this part of the country again, please drop by," Judd said.

John picked out buckskin. "This is the one I want," he said.

"John, let me give you a bill of sale."

"That won't be necessary as long as you are okay with the twenty dollars," John replied.

"That's fine with me," Judd replied. John said goodbye then rode off.

The second day it started to rain. John decided to camp along the river for the night, hoping for the rain to let up. The following morning John heard the sound of several riders coming toward him. John stood up as the riders surrounded his campsite.

"What can I do for you men?" John asked.

One of the men spoke up, "You can drop your gun belt and get your hands up, mister."

"I haven't done anything," John replied.

"Just shut up and listen. I think you know why we're here," replied one of the riders.

"What is your name, and where did you get that horse?"

"Frankly, it's none of your business! My name is John Crow, and I bought my horse from Mr. Raker at the Circle R two days ago," John replied.

"Let's see the bill of sale then," one of the men asked.

"I don't have one. Mr. Raker asked me if I wanted one, and I told him no. It didn't matter as long as he knew I paid for the horse," John answered.

"Well, that's what we thought. Not only did you rape and strangle Mr. Raker's daughter, you stole one of his horses too!" another man shouted.

"You must be a breed with a name like John Crow. Only someone like you would do such a terrible thing to a young girl," one of the other riders said.

"My mother was Comanche, and my father was in the US Cavalry. He was assigned to Bent's Fort. I swear I never saw the girl you are talking about, only Mr. Raker and his cook," John said.

"That's a helluva of a story, considering you were seen leaving the ranch in a big hurry on a Buckskin horse that evening just like the one you're riding," one of the men said.

"I never left the ranch in the evening. I left after lunch. It couldn't have been me," John replied.

"Boys, I think we've all heard enough of this man's lame excuses." By now all the riders had stepped down from their horses and had John surrounded.

"You know what we do with saddle tramps like you?" one of the men shouted. "We hang 'em."

One of the men, Tom, stepped forward and said, "Hanging is too good for this killer. I have a better idea. I want two of you to gather some firewood over here by the river's edge and build a fire. By the way, does anyone have a branding iron?"

"Ya, Tom. I have one in my saddlebags," one of the men shouted.

John was filled with fear; he tried to break through the circle of men, only to be knocked to the ground and held there waiting for further orders from Tom.

"After the fire burns down I want you to place the branding iron in the coals until it is white-hot. Then, we will be ready take care of this matter," Tom told everyone.

John's hands and feet had been tied together. Two men dragged him facedown near the fire. John was yelling at the top of his voice, "You are making a terrible mistake! I don't deserve this. At least take me back to Mr. Raker's ranch, and this whole matter can be cleared up."

"Okay, men, bring him over here next to the fire."

One of the other men handed Tom the branding iron.

"Hold him down just like you would if you were branding a calf!" Tom yelled.

John was writhing in agony as the red-hot iron was placed on his lower back. While John was screaming, two of the men rolled him over and branded the left side of his face. John passed out, and his body lied limp on the ground. One of the men took a rope off his saddle and tied it to his feet; he then dragged him out into the swift part of the river before cutting the rope loose, letting the current take John's tortured body downstream.

The riders mounted up, looked back momentarily, then rode off. They caught the right man and served their retribution. They were riding back to the Circle R and let Judd Raker know that it was over.

After riding back to the ranch Judd greeted the men in his usual way then invited them inside. Judd led the men into the parlor and asked them to sit down and tell him exactly what happened.

After hearing their story, Judd flew into a rage. "You fools, you killed the wrong man! I sold the man you described a buckskin horse, and he left after lunch the same day. He had nothing to do with my daughter's death that happened the next day! What the hell is wrong with you? You didn't even give the man a chance to defend himself," Judd explained.

"Well, sir, we asked him about the horse, and he told us he bought it from you but did not ask for a bill of sale. Since he fit the description we were sure we had the right man," Tom said.

"I offered him a bill of sale, but he didn't want it. You killed the wrong man. The real killer just rode off. You better get out of here and find the right man or don't come back. None of you will have a job!" Judd shouted in disgust.

Meanwhile, John's burnt body was rushing downstream until it entered a swell which led into a bank of dead trees. He was gasping for air; his clothes were blood soaked, and he was freezing. He lied against the fallen trees in the icy water, trying to catch his breath and rest for a while. He could only see the bank of the river on one side. He couldn't loosen the rope without injuring himself further. He gave up fighting the river. Exhaustion and loss of blood had taken over. His body lay motionless as the water churned rolling him back and forth. There was nothing John could do but hope that someone riding by might see him before he died; the sun would be setting soon. John wasn't sure, but he thought he heard the sound of wagon wheels in the distance. He was too weak to yell; he just lied there unable to utter a word.

Suddenly the wagon stopped, and a woman jumped down. She caught a glimpse of John as the sun reflected on his body in the water. The woman ran to the river's edge, but she could not reach John. She went back to the wagon and brought back a rope. She would have to lasso John as he could do nothing to help. After fighting to lasso John, she finally landed the large noose over his feet. She tied the other end to the wagon and had the horse pull until John was out of the water and was on the bank.

He was moaning as the flesh on raw areas where he was branded began to tear away while the horse slowly dragged him up onto the bank. By now John was in shock; he couldn't move nor speak. The woman tried frantically to remove the rope tied around John' body by cutting it in short pieces, trying not to injure John further. Finally she had removed the last section of rope, then she returned to the wagon. She brought back a blanket then covered John's body, trying to warm him up and stop the chilling.

Afterward, it took the woman over an hour to drag John's body close enough to load him in the wagon. She was finally able to get John upright and line him up against the back of the wagon, where she picked up his feet then slowly pushed his body into the wagon. It was late, and her father would be worried if she didn't get back to the ranch soon. Later that evening she arrived back at the ranch. After explaining what happened, two men took John into the parlor and laid him on a blanket on the floor face down, exposing the deep burn marks made by the branding iron on John's back.

"Who would do this to a man? He's been branded, and it is hard to see what the man looks like. I have never seen a person so disfigured like this, only by the Indians," her father said.

"Daddy, we need to take him upstairs and put him in the guest room until he gets better. I will watch after him," the daughter volunteered.

"Merced, that is up to you. We don't know how long he may be here. He could be here a few days or a couple of weeks if he doesn't die," her father said.

Merced changed the stranger's dressings each day and gave him food and water. She stayed with him day and night. After a week John started to murmur something. Merced bent over to hear what he was trying to say, but he was too weak to talk. The next morning the stranger began to show signs of movement and asked where he was.

"I am Merced. I am the one who pulled you out of the river. My father is Chris Fraser, and this is his ranch. And by the way, what is your name?"

"I am John Crow, and I appreciate your saving my life. I just don't remember much of anything else."

Merced went downstairs and asked her father to come up as the stranger was coherent and was able to talk.

Merced's father walked upstairs and said, "I am Chris, and your name is?"

"I am John Crow, and I appreciate everything you and your daughter have done for me. I don't know how I'll ever be able to repay you for all you've done."

"Don't worry about that, son. You just need to get some rest, and we will talk again later when you are up to it," Chris said.

Several days later, John felt well enough to walk downstairs and join the others for breakfast.

During breakfast Chris asked, "Who did this to you and why?"

After John explained what happened, no one could understand why those angry men wanted to kill him without any real evidence and without giving him a chance to prove his innocence.

John spoke up, "Those men ruined my life. I can't even stand to look at my face in the mirror. I swear to God I will find out who did this to me and who raped and murdered Mr. Raker's daughter if it takes me the rest of my life."

"I understand, John. It was a terrible thing those men did to you, but you just can't take the law into your own hands, or you will be no better than those men that did this. So what are your plans, John?"

"The first thing I'm going to do is ride back to Mr. Raker and show him what happened to me and find out more about his daughter and who may have killed her."

Merced interrupted, "I don't think you are well enough to ride that far. Why don't you stay here a few more days?"

"Thanks for everything. I can't stay longer. I have to leave as soon as I get my gear together," John replied.

After saying his goodbyes John rode off toward the Circle R. Two days later, John arrived at the Circle R ranch house and tied his horse up in front. Judd heard him ride up and came out to greet him. He recognized the buckskin but John.

"What can I do for you, mister?" Judd shouted.

"Well, you probably don't recognize me, but I am John Crow. I am terribly sorry to hear about your daughter," John said sorrowfully.

"I didn't recognize you, John, but thank you for your kind remarks. I thought my men had killed you. Thank God you are still alive. Please come inside," Judd said.

"No thanks to your men, but somehow I survived with the help of a young woman driving by in a buckboard."

"I know what happened to you was a terrible thing. I'm not sure if I can ever make it up to you, son, but somehow I will try. Please don't blame my men. It was my fault," Judd said. Judd was sickened by the loss of his only daughter and by what happened to John because of her death. The two men sat outside on the porch and discussed everything at length.

John asked, "Who told you the killer left on a buckskin and gave you my description?"

"It was one of the newer hands. He had been here a couple of weeks. He was the one who told everyone it was you who killed my daughter then rode off on the buckskin. I didn't put the whole story together until a day later. There was something wrong! The man's name was Will Shephard, and he suddenly left the next day after my daughter was killed."

"Mr. Raker, I think Will Shephard killed your daughter and used me for a scapegoat. He had seen me the day before when we first met. It makes perfect sense, don't you think? I became the alibi, and the description fit as no one else knew exactly when I was here at the ranch. Everyone was convinced even the next day after I left."

"You know, John, what you said makes a lot of sense. Will was the only one here, and it was easy for him to blame everything on you and leave before anyone figured out what happened."

"Mr. Raker, do you have any idea which direction Will may have taken?"

"I didn't know much about the man, but he did mention that he had a brother living somewhere around Santa Fe and that he had not seen him for several years."

"I believe I know what I need to do, and that is to find Will and bring him back, so that he can stand trial for murder."

"A killer like that is too good to hang. He should be shot on sight. In fact if you can provide us with proof he is dead, it would be worth ten thousand dollars to me just knowing he will never rape or kill again," Judd said sternly.

John asked, "Can you give me a description of the man?"

"Well, he had a medium build with blonde hair. He has a scar over his right eye, and he wears a dirty old Stetson with a wide brim. I guess he is about thirty years old," Judd replied.

"Thanks for the information, and I'll be on my way."

John was on the trail for two days when he rode into the small town of Plainesville. He decided to inquire around about the man he was looking for, but no one had seen him.

A young boy overhearing the conversation spoke up. "Mister, I saw a man with a scar like the one you told about," the young boy said.

John walked over to the boy and asked him several questions.

"Do you remember what kind of horse the man was riding?" John asked.

The boy spoke up, "He was riding a black horse with a white mane. He left town that way," pointing to the east.

"I am much obliged, son," John said as he threw the boy a silver dollar. The young boy picked up the dollar and grinned ear to ear.

"Thank you, mister, and good luck!" the boy yelled as John rode off.

John knew he was on the right trail, and it would be just matter of time before he caught up with the killer. The real concern was that to get to Santa Fe, he had to ride through Comanche country. John thought about this matter carefully but decided to continue on. Somehow he had to clear his name.

That morning John rode toward a canyon with bluffs on each side. He knew this would be risky at best; perhaps he would ride into an ambush. As he reached the canyon entrance he stayed in the shadows. John rode cautiously through the canyon until he reached the open space on the other side. He kept looking for sign of the Comanche but saw nothing. Far ahead he spotted a small stand of trees, where he was hoping to find water. Neither he nor his horse could last much longer without water.

John rode slowly toward the trees, then he saw a small pond to the left. Cautiously stepping down from his horse, he looked around for any sign of the Comanche. He took his hat off and filled it with water; he gave his horse a drink then lay down on the bank and quenched his own thirst. John didn't want his horse to bloat, so he pulled him away from the water. After a short rest and filling his canteen John knew he couldn't stay any longer; this was the only source of water for miles around.

John mounted up and continued across the prairie. In the distance he could see smoke rising. *It must be Comanche*, John thought, as he carefully approached the burning buildings that were coming into sight. This was all that remained of a way station. The Comanche had ridden off, leaving death and destruction behind. John approached the smoldering buildings when he saw three scattered bodies burnt beyond recognition. John stepped down from his horse to see if there were any survivors. He was startled by the sound of a weakened voice. He turned to the side and saw a man tied to a wagon wheel, barely alive.

"What happened?" John asked.

The man motioned for John to come closer. John bent over and noticed the scar over the man's right eye and what was left of his blonde hair. This was the man he had been trailing. The man told him that he had spent the night with a family who lived nearby and planned on going to Santa Fe the next morning. Early that morning the Comanche came riding down on the way station, and everyone here were yelling and screaming. They killed everything in sight, then they set fire to the way station. They took two young women with them and left the rest behind.

"You must be Will Shephard. I've been tracking you for days. I was told you were the man who raped and killed Judd Raker's daughter. I just want the truth. After looking closer John noticed than man's eyes had been burned out.

"I am Will Shephard, and I am a dead man. There is no use for me to lie about the killing. It was Judd's brother, Allen, who killed his daughter. He came in late one night drunk and saw a light on in the barn where Carrie, Judd's daughter, was doing something with a new colt. Allen tried to reach out and grab Carrie, but she slapped his face. She screamed, but no one heard her. That's when Allen backhanded her, knocking her to the ground. He apparently raped her then strangled her when she refuse to let him have his way. Afterward, Allen ran to the house and told Judd what he had done. Judd was distraught over his daughter's death but was more concerned about his family's image in the territory."

"So what happened to Allen?"

"Judd gave him five hundred dollars and told him to pack up and leave the territory until this whole matter calmed down. The next morning one of the hands found Allen hanging from one of the rafters in the barn with the money sticking out of his pockets. Apparently after Allen sobered up he couldn't handle the humiliation and hanged himself."

John said, "I would like to ask you one more question."

He turned to Will, but it was too late—he was dead. John knew what he had to do. He and Will had been set up by Judd himself to hide the truth about Judd's brother. John would have to take the word of a dying man who had nothing to gain by lying, and deal with Judd himself. Everything started to make more sense; that's why Judd wanted John to kill the alleged killer rather than bring him back to stand trial.

After burying Will and what was left of the other charred bodies, John started the long trek back to Judd Raker's ranch. Following several days on the trail John decided to report what happened to the territorial marshal and have him ride in with him to confront Judd Raker. The nearest marshal's office was about twenty miles from Judd Raker's ranch, located in the small town of Red Creek.

John arrived in Red Creek looking for the marshal's office. It was on the other side of the street. John rode over to the marshal's office then walked inside and introduced himself. After telling his story to Jim Taylor, the marshal, the marshal looked at John in disbelief but didn't question the truth of the story.

"You know, mister, that's the damnedest story I believe I've ever heard. The only reason I believe you is that it would be impossible to make up something like that," the marshal replied.

"Marshal, Judd Raker's ranch is a good day's ride. Will you ride out with me in case there is trouble?" John asked.

"Ya, I'll ride out with you. We'll leave at sunup. I will meet you down the street at the livery stable," the marshal said.

Early the next morning John and the marshal rode out together.

"There's one thing, John. When we get to the ranch let me handle everything. I don't want you killing anyone!" the marshal warned.

"Okay, but I want the truth, or I swear I'll beat it out of Judd Raker for what he did to me," John said.

It was late afternoon when John and the marshal arrived at the ranch. They cautiously approached the ranch house. Judd saw them coming, and in his usual way, he stepped out on the porch and greeted the men.

"What can I do for you, fellows?" Judd asked.

John spoke up, "I think you know what we want!"

"I am Jim Taylor, United States Marshal out of Red Creek. You are under arrest for conspiracy and for falsifying information against two men being charged with murder. I am taking you back to Red Creek to stand trial."

Beads of sweat began to roll off Judd's face.

"You don't understand, Marshal. I couldn't let my brother take the blame for my daughter's murder. It would destroy our family's reputation."

"What gives you the right to frame two innocent men for what your own brother did?" the marshal asked.

"It just made sense at the time. I am terribly sorry for what I have done. Please let me go inside and gather some of my belongings to take with me," Judd asked.

"Make it quick," the marshal replied.

John was facing the porch, and the marshal had his back turned tying down his saddlebags when suddenly a shot rang out. Judd came out of the house shooting. The first shot struck the marshal in the shoulder. Before Judd got off another shot, John drew his gun and shot Judd twice. Judd fell down the stairs to the ground. John walked over to make sure he was dead. He prodded him with a boot; Judd didn't move. He was dead.

"Let someone else bury him. I'm tired of burying people." Then John turned to the marshal and asked, "Are you all right?"

"I think I'll be okay. The bullet went through the fleshy side of my shoulder."

"Here, Marshal. Let me tie my scarf around your shoulder to stop the bleeding." John cinched it up tight and then helped the marshal on his horse.

"Do you think you can make it back to Red Creek, Marshal?"

"You know, John, I believe I'll be all right. And one more thing. When you buy another horse, get a bill of sale."

John replied with a smile on his face, "I'll do that."

JESSIE SUTTER

"Mr. Franklin, I would like to withdraw all my money. How much time do you need?"

"Jessie, please give me a couple of days. But why are you taking all your money out of my bank? Did we do something to upset you?" Buck Franklin, the bank president, replied.

"No, sir, it is nothing like that. I have decided to move to the Colorado territory and take up ranching."

"What do you know about ranching, and what are you going to do with your holdings here in Detroit?"

"I am going to learn the ropes of ranching when I get to Colorado. I am turning everything over to Everett Runyon, my nephew. You've met him. He's been into your bank with me on several occasions. He's the clean-cut young man who speaks proper English and is extremely polite," Jessie replied.

"Well, I must say, I am not only surprised but shocked to see you leave this part of the country. You will be missed by everyone, for sure," Buck said.

"Before I leave town I will properly introduce my nephew to you so that he may continue to do business here," Jessie stated.

Following the travel arrangements and packing, Jessie was prepared to take the six-week stagecoach ride to Colorado Springs. It was the most difficult way of traveling Jessie had ever experienced. He wasn't accustomed to the rough rutted roads, the weather, and the dust blowing inside the stagecoach. The fourth day the stagecoach was stopped by a small bank of Indians looking for someone who wasn't on the stagecoach. The driver gave the Indians two bottles of whiskey, then they rode off.

"Since we're stopped, this looks like a good place to get out and stretch your legs for a few minutes. The next part of the ride is a long, slow, and bumpy ride over the mountains," the driver said.

After everyone had gotten out and stretched their limbs it was time to get back inside and continue on. It began to rain, and the horses worked hard to pull the stagecoach up the steep mountain side. The road became so slick the horses couldn't pull the stagecoach and riders without sliding backward. The drive yelled for the horses to stop.

"Everyone get out. You'll have to walk the next mile or so. It's just too much for the horses. You might want to put your raingear on if you have any. It gets cold and windy up here."

After reaching the summit everyone climbed back on the stage and continued on. Jessie's stomach began to ache, and he was near exhaustion. He had never felt this way before.

"I don't know if it's the elevation or the ride, but I feel like I could go to sleep for two days," Jessie commented. One of the women sitting by the window suggested she change places with Jessie, allowing him to get more air. About an hour later he began to feel better.

"Ma'am, I want to thank you for allowing me to sit by the window. It helped a lot," Jessie said.

"It's quite all right. I hope you are feeling better," she replied.

Jessie nodded, indicating he was feeling better.

The next three weeks were grueling, covering some of the most remote and hostile land anyone could cross. The stage pulled up to a way station for the night. All the passengers got out except for Jessie.

Jack, the shotgun rider, stuck his head inside and asked, "Mister, are you all right?"

"Yes, I am fine. I was just doing some thinking, that's all," Jessie replied.

Later Jessie climbed out of the stagecoach and walked inside where everyone was sitting around a large dining table eating rabbit stew.

"Just grab a seat, mister, and I will get you a bowl of rabbit stew," the cook said.

"I have never tasted rabbit. Is this a specialty dish or just something that everyone eats out here?" Jessie asked.

The cook laughed. "You know, mister, I don't think rabbit is a specialty dish since they run wild out here. Some people like it better than chicken though."

"Go ahead, then. I will try a bowl of the stew," Jessie replied. "This is really good, especially for something wild."

The next morning the stage driver yelled at everyone to get back on the stage as it would be another long day. The following two weeks were uneventful, just dealing with the weather and rutted roadway. Early one morning to the north rising above the valley was smoke. It was difficult to tell from where it was coming. Two hours later the stagecoach came upon the smoke still curling into the air. As the stage approached the smoky area, it became apparent that there had been a woodhouse and barn that were still burning what was left of the way station.

The driver stopped the stagecoach about fifty yards away from the burning buildings "Everyone stay inside. Come on, Herb!" he yelled. "Grab your rifle and come with me. Let's take a closer look."

Both men cautiously approached the burning structure with rifles cocked, looking for any sign of life or what might have happened. In the corner of the burnt-out cabin was a small child with a tomahawk buried in her back. A man still sitting in a smoldering rocking chair had several arrows protruding from his chest. On the ground about twenty feet away, just outside the burning structure, lied a woman who had been scalped while trying to escape. There were no sign of life, only carnage. Both men slowly walked back to the passengers who were still on the stagecoach.

Before anything could be said, one of the passengers asked, "Did you find anything out there?"

"The driver spoke up, "We saw more than I wished we had. We are going to move on. We can't stay here for the night."

"What did you see? Some dead bodies or what? We need to know. It could affect all of us," one of the passengers said.

"None of you need to see anything there. It will make you sick. There were three bodies that had been mutilated. That's all I'm going to tell you," the stage driver said.

The stage pulled out past the burning structures. There was no time to bury the dead; the stagecoach needed to get as far away as possible before making camp for the night. At about ten o'clock they came to a river where they stopped for the night. The driver removed two ropes on top of the stagecoach, holding tents and other supplies in place. He dropped the two tents down over the side to the shot gun rider.

"We'll pitch the tents by the river!" the driver yelled. "Some of you will have to double up. I am sorry we don't have better accommodations for you folks," he said.

The women shared one tent, and the men took the other one. The driver and shotgun rider would stand watch for the night. Morning came with no sign of Indians. It had rained so hard the bridge over the river had been washed away. The driver told everyone they would have to find a place to cross the river. The shotgun rider volunteered to walk down the river and check for a place to cross. An hour later he returned.

"I found a place about half a mile downstream. I think we can cross there," he said.

After loading everything back on the stagecoach, the driver rode downstream to the crossing area.

"Okay, everyone, make sure you stay in your seats and don't let the doors open no matter what happens," the driver instructed.

The stagecoach entered the water, and the horses working hard pulled the stagecoach and passengers across the river without a problem. Jessie was caught up in the scenery of the rolling hills and prairie. He had never witnessed anything like this before. Jessie was born and raised in Detroit. This was the first time he had ever left the city. The woman giving Jessie her seat was a woman named Millie Sledge. She was going back to Colorado Springs after having visited her mother in Flint, Michigan.

"My name is Mildred, but my friends call me Millie," she said as she asked Jessie what his name was.

"They call me Jessie. I am from Detroit. I have always wanted to come west and become a cattle rancher," he told Millie.

"What you know about ranching?" Millie asked.

"I don't know anything about ranching. I have always been intrigued by the possibility, though."

"It's interesting you would bring up the subject of ranching. My brother has a small spread east of Colorado Springs that he has wanted to sell. This might be something you may want to consider," Millie suggested.

Jessie had near met a woman who was so comfortable to be around. This is the type of woman he could possibly spend the rest of his life with. Though they just met, Jessie had grown fond of Millie already. She was the kind of woman Jessie pictured in his mind—a strong, take-charge type with deep feelings and nurturing ways about her.

"I would like to know more about your brother's ranch and take a look at it when we get to Colorado Springs," Jessie replied.

There was something about Jessie that intrigued Millie. He was very pleasant to talk to, but he knew little about living in the west. Millie had never been married and had never given much thought marrying a man who was not from the west. Over the next two weeks of traveling Millie was beginning to fall in love with Jessie. Both seemed to have a lot in common. Their ideals and dreams were similar. Jessie was extremely kind and intelligent. Jessie was an easy person to talk to; he was very open and unpretentious.

The stage finally arrived in Colorado Springs without further complications.

"Where would you suggest I stay, Millie?" Jessie asked.

"Jessie, there is a good hotel called the Penrose just down the street from the stage stop. The rooms are clean, and the service is good."

"Thanks, Millie. I appreciate your suggestions. By the way, when could we ride out to your brother's ranch?"

"How about tomorrow? I will bring the buckboard at about eight o'clock, and we can leave then," Millie suggested.

The next morning Millie met Jessie in front of the hotel.

"Oh, there is one more thing. You can't be seen on the ranch wearing those clothes. We are going over to the mercantile to buy you some clothes suitable for this part of the country," Millie said.

"I suppose you're right," Jessie replied.

After Jessie was fitted for jeans, a western shirt, hat, and boots, they were ready to leave. They rode to her brother's ranch about five miles east of town. As they approached the ranch the wagon passed through a large log gate with a hanging sign bearing the name the Doubled Slash *S* Ranch.

"I thought you said this was a small ranch! It looks like it goes on forever," Jessie commented.

"Jessie, it is small by comparison to others in the area. My brother's ranch is only ten thousand acres." They were now in front of the ranch house. Jessie jumped down then helped Millie off the wagon. They went inside and met Millie's brother.

"Jessie, this is my brother, Frank Sledge. Frank, this is Jessie Sutter from Detroit."

"Nice to meet you, Jessie," Frank said as he extended his arm to shake hands.

"The pleasure is mine," Jessie replied.

Millie and her brother took Jessie on a ride, covering the entire ranch. Jessie thought it was the most beautiful setting he had ever seen. After much negotiation Frank and Jessie came to an agreement. Jesse agreed to purchase the ranch with the understanding that Frank and his men would stay on for one year, allowing Jessie time to learn about ranching.

One afternoon Millie and Jessie took a buggy ride to a nearby river to have a picnic.

While sitting on a blanket under an old cottonwood tree, Jessie asked Millie to marry him, and she accepted. Their plan following the wedding was to honeymoon in nearby Manitou Springs. This way Jessie would not be too far away from his ranch.

After the picnic, Jessie complained about severe stomach pain and being extremely tired.

"Why don't I help you into the buggy, and I will drive back to the ranch," Millie suggested.

Millie helped Jessie himself up into the buggy. He lied back in the seat resting until Millie got back to the ranch. Upon arriving at the ranch Millie yelled for someone to help her get Jessie inside the house. Two men took Jessie upstairs and laid him on the large log bed. Jessie had already passed out. Millie knew something was wrong. These were the same symptoms Jessie had experienced on his way to Colorado Springs. Millie sent for the doctor who arrived at the ranch about two hours later. He asked everyone to leave the room until he had time to evaluate Jessie. Jessie's blood pressure was low, and he had severe abdominal pains. The doctor left some pills for Jessie and told him to take them every two to three hours for his stomach pain as needed, and to rest for a few days until he got his strength back.

Millie asked, "What do you think the problem is?"

"You know, I'm not sure. It could be several things. His blood pressure is too low, and it needs to get back up into a normal range. And with the severe stomach pain, it could be his diet or fatigue. I suggest you feed him lots of protein and make sure he gets plenty of bed rest. I want to see him in my office in one week if he feels better. Otherwise, let me know, and I will come back to the ranch and check on him."

After several days Jessie was back on his feet, feeling as well as ever.

The wedding date had been set for the following week. The week of the wedding came, and Millie and Jessie were married. It was a large gathering of people coming from as far away as Denver and Pueblo, Colorado. Following the reception and service they left for Manitou Springs, where they stayed in the Cliff House during their honeymoon. Everything was going along well with Jessie and Millie adjusting to married life back at the ranch. Jessie was becoming educated about the livestock and how to manage the ranch hands.

One afternoon Millie and Jessie rode into Colorado Springs for supplies. Jessie pulled up the wagon alongside the general store.

"Jessie and Millie, it's nice to see you two! How is married life treating you anyway?" Bart Lebaron, the store owner, asked.

"Life is good," Jessie said, and Millie shook her head in agreement.

Jessie pulled out a list of items they needed at the ranch and handed it to Bart.

"It will take me a while to fill the order. Why don't you two go across the street and have a cool drink and get out of the hot sun? When I have your wagon loaded I will send for you," Bart said.

"Okay!"

An hour later the wagon was loaded when Bart sent his son over to the saloon to let Jessie and Millie know.

"Tell your dad we will be right out, after we finish these drinks," Jessie said. Jessie and Millie were ready leave the saloon. Jessie had just stepped outside when he heard gunshots. They were coming from the bank across the street.

"Millie, get back inside, and I will be back after I find out what's going on!"

Millie yelled for Jessie to stay back as she followed him out onto the street. Suddenly two men came out of the bank with gunshots ringing out. Jessie turned toward Millie, but before he could say another word, he was shot in the back. Jessie fell to the ground with Millie falling on top. Millie screamed for someone to get the doc.

The two outlaws rode out of town before the sheriff and his men could get to them. The doc came running across the street where Jessie way lying. The doc rolled Jessie over and checked his vitals. It was too late; Jessie was gone.

Millie cried; she was grief stricken. She had never loved anyone like Jessie, who was the love of her life. It seemed to Millie that she and Jessie had spent a lifetime together, not just a few weeks. The doc reached over and laid his hand on Millie's shoulder; he told her that he just found out that Jessie was dying of a rare illness called Addison's disease and that he would have lived but a few months.

MADELINE MCQUINN

Madeline was raised in an aristocratic home. Her father was a medical doctor, and her mother was a socialite. Madeline was raised in St. Louis, and she remained there after the Civil War. She was a petite woman with auburn hair down to her waist. Her eyes were dark brown, and her lightly tanned face had a few scattered freckles. Madeline was not only attractive but was also intelligent. She had been educated in the best schools, but she grew up spoiled. Her father gave her anything she wanted. As she grew older she was inexcusably demanding. She expected the best and settled for nothing less.

Madeline was adventuresome from the time she was a little girl. Following the death of her father and mother she decided to go west and explore the frontier. She boarded a train in St. Louis bound for the Wyoming Territory. It would require that she change trains and finish her travels by stagecoach from Denver.

After boarding the train a young man asked her if he could take a seat beside her. He was middle aged, with a neatly trimmed beard. His features were striking with dark combed-back hair. He had a hook for his left hand.

"Why, I suppose so. It looks like there are plenty of other seats on this train," Madeline quipped.

"I am sorry, ma'am, but I thought you might want some company since you are traveling alone. By the way, my name is Hunter Smith. And yours, ma'am?"

"I really don't feel like sharing my name with you, since we have not been formally introduced," Madeline said in a sarcastic tone.

"I am sorry, ma'am. Pardon the intrusion. I'll take a seat over there," he said as he pointed to a seat across the aisle.

"Oh, I guess it's all right. You may sit here if you like. I am sorry. I guess I am just tired. By the way, my name is Madeline Mcquinn."

After a short conversation Hunter pulled the brim of his hat down over his eyes and fell asleep. The train stopped to take on water and to let the passengers stretch their legs. "Well, folks this is as far as we go. The next train to Denver will arrive sometime tomorrow!" the conductor shouted.

The following morning Madeline was boarding the train when Hunter said, "May I help you, ma'am?"

Madeline turned, and seeing who it was, she said, "If you wish!" There was something about Hunter that Madeline was intrigued by. Maybe it was his manners or his striking features; she wasn't sure.

Back on the train, Madeline seemed more amicable and willing to talk. Hunter told her he was going to Laramie to do business as a cattle broker, and then he would return to St. Louis. Hunter's wife had died of cholera two years before.

"I am sorry to hear of your loss, Mr. Smith," Madeline said.

"It's all right. And please call me Hunter."

Madeline had never been married and was in her late twenties. Madeline felt badly about how she had treated Hunter on the train and decided to give him a chance.

"I suppose you are wondering how I lost my hand! It happened at the end of the war. My regiment was trying to take a hill back from the Yankees. We charged the hill but didn't know there were over three hundred soldiers waiting in the trees at the top of the hill. I heard a charge command, and horse soldiers came at us from all sides. I had my rifle and bayonet pointing up in front of me when a soldier on horseback charged me, taking off my hand with his saber at the same time I fired. His horse jumped over me, but the soldier fell on top of me. When I came to I realized I had killed my own brother, who was lying dead on top of me. It was a difficult time. My brother was against slavery, and I decided to fight on the other side."

"I am terribly sorry, I did not mean to intrude into your personal life," Madeline said.

Hunter looked up at Madeline without saying another word. The two just set there staring out the window, waiting for the train to pull into Denver. Late that afternoon the train arrived. The next day Hunter would take the stagecoach to Laramie.

Madeline approached Hunter and asked, "You know, Hunter, this is the first time I have been west. What kind of town is Laramie, anyway?"

"Laramie is a rough town. It has changed since the railroad came through. It attracted people from all over—gunmen, cattle rustlers, gamblers, and the like."

"It sounds intriguing. Maybe I should go there," Madeline said.

"I'm not sure it's a proper place for a lady of your upbringing. Of course, it is your choice."

"Hunter, I've decided to ride with you to Laramie and check out the town," Madeline said.

"That's your choice. I'll be staying at the Laramie House, so if you need anything while I am there, please let me know," Hunter offered.

The coach was loaded and was on its way. The first stop would be in Fort Collins. Following a two-hour layover, the stage left for Laramie. It was the last leg of the trip. About an hour out gunshots were heard. Joe, the driver, whipped the horses, forcing them to run as hard as they could. Another shot rang out, and Mel, riding shotgun, fell from the coach. Joe knew he couldn't outrun the outlaws and started to rein in the team.

"What's happening?" Madeline asked.

"It looks like we're being held up," Hunter replied.

"Whoa!" Joe said, bringing the horses to a stop. Four outlaws had caught up with the stage, and they asked everyone to get out.

One of the men stepped up and opened the stage door. "Okay, everyone get out and empty your pockets into my hat. I want all of your money and any valuables."

After stepping outside Hunter reached inside his pocket to pull out his pocket watch, and another man drew and shot him in the chest. He fell to the ground.

"Why did you shoot him? He doesn't even carry a gun!" Madeline screamed out.

"Miss, if he lives, he might want to carry one," the outlaw said in a laughing voice.

Madeline fell to the ground over Hunter, cradling him in her arms. "Somebody do something, or he will die," she said. She was sobbing; she knew now she had fallen in love with Hunter, and she didn't want him to die. Madeline tore off part of her blouse and sopped up the blood then tucked it inside Hunter's shirt. The outlaws left, leaving everyone standing on the old rutted road.

Joe hurried over to Hunter and said, "Help me get him inside the coach. He's lost a lot of blood."

Madeline climbed in first, holding Hunter's head in her lap. Everyone boarded the coach and continued their trip to Laramie. The stage arrived in Laramie with Hunter still unconscious.

Joe pulled up in front of the stage depot and yelled, "I need help! A man has been shot."

Several men rushed to the stagecoach and helped carry Hunter to Doc Wilson's office across the street. They pounded on the door, and the doctor finally opened it.

"We have a man badly hurt. Where can we lay him? Joe asked.

"Bring him over here and lay him on the table," the doctor replied.

Madeline followed then men into the doctor's office. "Will he be all right," Madeline asked.

"Young woman, I don't know. He has a bullet buried in his chest. I won't know anything until I get it out," the doctor replied.

"I will wait here until you get the bullet out," Madeline said.

"No, you must all leave. As soon as I know something I will let you know," Doc Wilson replied.

Madeline waited all night outside the doc's office. Madeline was sitting on the boardwalk asleep against a window sill. Early the next morning Doc Wilson came out and gave Madeline a report on Hunter.

"Miss, wake up, I have some news for you," the doc said while shaking her shoulder. Madeline suddenly woke up.

"Is everything all right?" Madeline asked.

"Yes, young lady. I think your friend is going to be all right. He is going to need a lot of care, though," the doc said.

"I will care for him," Madeline said.

"He will need to stay here for another week before he could be be moved," the doc explained.

Madeline made arrangements for a room at the Laramie House. Hunter had told her on the train that was where he usually stayed. The following week Hunter was well enough to be moved. Madeline summoned two men to help her take Hunter to the Laramie House. Each day Madeline attended to Hunter's wound, giving him the best of care. Two weeks had passed, and Hunter was able to sit up and walk by himself.

"Now that you are feeling better, how long will you be in Laramie?" Madeline asked.

"I will be here for about a week before I return to St. Louis," Hunter replied.

"I think you need more time to get your strength back. Don't you think it would be a good idea to stay a little longer?" Madeline asked.

"I was under the impression that you didn't care about me either way, but I do want to thank you for taking care of me," Hunter replied.

"That's not true. I am sorry that I gave you the wrong impression. In fact, I would like to get to know you better," Madeline said.

Hunter was excited, and he wanted to spend more time with her. He was falling in love with this independent high-spirited woman who had cared for him so long.

"I will stay for another week before I leave for St. Louis," Hunter replied.

The two walked up and down Main Street hand in hand, as if they were newlyweds. Hunter had never met a woman as beautiful and exciting as Madeline. Within a few days Madeline was sharing her excitement and love with Hunter. She did not want him to leave.

"Why don't you stay, and we'll get married?" Madeline asked.

"You are asking me to marry you. We really don't know each other that well," Hunter replied.

Madeline said, "Yes, I have fallen in love with you."

"I feel like I've known you all my life, and I feel the same way Hunter said in an excited voice. Without further hesitation, Hunter accepted Madeline's marriage proposal.

"I still need to go back to St. Louis to wrap up my business affairs. Maybe you should go with me," Hunter asked.

"I understand, but I just want you by my side, that's all. I will be all right here until you get back," Madeline said.

"Are you sure you will be all right here alone in a strange town?"

"I will stay at the Laramie House until you return, and then we can plan the wedding and decide where we want to live."

"Don't worry. I will manage to stay busy while you are away," Madeline said.

"I suppose if you are comfortable with this arrangement, I will try to get back as soon as I can. I will leave you some money to live on while I'm gone," Hunter replied.

"Hunter, that won't be necessary. I am financially able to take care of myself," Madeline replied.

By now, everyone in town could see Madeline and Hunter were very much in love, and they appeared very happy together. Hunter was as happy as he had ever been. Madeline shared in his love and excitement, too.

It was 8:00 a.m., and the stage to Denver was ready to leave. Hunter had loaded his suit cases on the stage and gave Madeline a big hug and kiss.

"I will miss you, darling!" Madeline shouted.

"I love you and will think of you every day," Hunter said as the stage pulled out.

Knowing Hunter would be gone for some time Madeline decided to look for something to keep her occupied. By now Madeline had met nearly everyone in town and was a pleasant addition. After several days she became bored and decided to go in the Prairie Saloon. Madeline had never drunk whiskey, only Sarsaparilla. Walking through the saloon doors she caught everyone's attention. She walked up to the bar and crowded in between the men.

"What can I do for you, little lady?" the bartender asked.

"I would like a whiskey," Madeline said. The men standing beside her offered to buy her a drink, but she declined.

The bartender said, "You know, this is no place for a lady."

The men were fighting their way to get to the bar. Everyone offered to buy Madeline a drink. A proper-looking man invited her to have a seat at his table. For some strange reason Madeline accepted.

"Excuse me, but what is a fine-looking woman doing in a place like this?" he asked.

"Thanks for the drink, mister, but that's none of your business," Madeline said as she got up from the table and walked out.

Everywhere Madeline went men would flock around. She was the best-looking woman seen in this part of the country in years. Madeline became bored and decided to look for something to do until Hunter returned. Madeline was in the saloon having a drink, standing across from the bartender.

"You look like you're a thousand miles away," the bartender said.

"Sam, I suppose I am. I am getting bored just walking around this little town with nothing to do but wait."

"Maybe you should get a part-time job to take up your time," Sam suggested.

"You know, Sam, that's exactly what I need something to keep myself busy until Hunter gets back. Thanks for the suggestion. I think I will check around town and see if anyone needs help," Madeline said.

Several days passed with no success in finding a job.

One of the men who frequented the saloon where Madeline happened to be said, "Pardon me, ma'am, but I overheard you talking to Sam the other night. My name is Elliott, and I understand you are looking for a job."

"That's right. I am, "Madeline replied.

"You might want to go over to Miss Holly's place. She is always looking for someone," Elliot suggested.

"I'll do just that. Thank you for the suggestion, mister."

Madeline walked down the street to a large two-story building with two balconies overlooking Main Street. The building was beautiful with a high-pitched roof painted in white and trimmed in bright red. Everyone could see the building from anywhere in town. Madeline walked over to Miss Holly's place and went in.

"May I help you, ma'am?" came a voice from across the room.

"I am looking for Miss Holly. Is she available?" Madeline asked.

"You've found her. I am Miss Holly. What can I do for you?" she replied.

"I was looking for work and someone said you may be looking for someone."

"What kind of work were you thinking of," Miss Holy inquired.

"To be honest, I don't even know what you do here," Madeline replied.

"I guess you could say we run a personal relations and entertainment business."

"I noticed all the women standing around when I came in. What do they do?" Madeline asked.

"They work in both areas on a private basis primarily by appointment. Occasionally we get walk-ins, especially on a Saturday night."

"I'm still not sure what it is you do, but I am very interested in a job," Madeline said.

"Madeline, I'll tell you what. If you want to start in the front here handling all of the appointment for the ladies, you may start immediately," Miss Holly said.

Madeline accepted the job, and after several days, she realized many of the important townspeople came in on a regular basis asking for the same woman. Though Madeline had never worked in a brothel she finally figured out what type of business Miss Holly ran.

One morning Miss Holly approached Madeline and said, "You know, Madeline, the real money is made upstairs. I know you would do well and make a lot more money than I can afford to pay you for booking appointments!"

"But Miss Holly, I am to be married when Hunter returns. What would he say if he found out," Madeline asked.

"He doesn't need to find out, and it would give you a chance to build up a few dollars on your own so that you could enjoy a nice honeymoon. Besides, there is no reason for Hunter to find out. We won't say anything about what you are doing here," Miss Holly replied.

"Well, I guess I will try it for a few days, but only until Hunter gets back," Madeline said.

"Oh, there's one more thing. Madeline, you will have to move in here so that you are readily available for clients," Missy Holly said. Madeline agreed to move in until Hunter returned.

Three weeks later Madeline received a telegram from Hunter, telling her he would be back the following week and that he missed her terribly. Madeline told Miss Holly she would be leaving in a few days because Hunter was arriving. Madeline checked back in the Laramie House as if she had never left.

The day Hunter was to arrive, the stage pulled into town about two hours late. Madeline became concerned but waited impatiently to greet Hunter. The stage finally arrived, and all the passengers got out. Hunter was the last person to climb down. Madeline ran to him with open arms and greeted him with a kiss.

"I thought I may never see you again, my love," Hunter said. Hunter picked Madeline up and whirled her around, holding on as to never let her go. That evening they settled in to their quarters at the Laramie House.

"So what have you been doing while I've been away," Hunter asked.

"Not much. Just doing odd jobs here and there, that's all. Let's talk about you and your trip. Did you have any problems on the way?" Madeline asked.

"No. Fortunately, my trip was uneventful, just the way I like it. I am so glad to see you again. You were always on my mind. I missed you so much," Hunter said.

"You look tired. Why don't you go next door and have a couple of drinks while I unpack everything? I'm sure you will be more relaxed," Madeline suggested.

Hunter excused himself and went next door to the saloon. He walked up to the bar and ordered a drink.

Sam, the bartender, said, "It's good to have you back. I hope your trip was a success."

"Thanks, Sam. It was. It doesn't look like much has changed around here," Hunter commented.

Someone sitting at one of the tables shouted to Hunter, "You should really keep a better eye on your fiancée. I'm sure the two of you will have a great honeymoon!" Everyone in the room started to laugh.

"What's so damned funny anyway?" Hunter asked.

"Why don't you go down the street and ask Miss Holly what your fiancée has been doing while you were away?"

Sam said, "Don't pay any attention. That man is drunk. He's just trying to stir things up."

"Sam, what did I miss? What happened while I was away? Don't lie to me. I need to know!" Hunter shouted.

"Hunter, I am sorry that everything turned out the way it did. I know you were happy and were planning on getting married when you got back. I don't want to be the one to ruin your dreams, but the cowboy who spoke up was right. You need to talk to Miss Holly, and then you can decide for yourself what you want to do," Sam said.

Hunter ran out of the saloon next door to ask Madeline what was going on. Hunter was upset and humiliated. He had no idea what had happened while he was away. Everyone in town knew something had happened but him. Hunter went upstairs and threw open the door.

"Madeline, I want to know what's been going on. What have you been doing since I left? Don't lie to me. I want the truth!" Hunter shouted.

"What are you talking about? I don't know what was said at the saloon, but you need to calm down," Madeline said.

"Were you working for Miss Holly? Yes or no?"

"Well, as a matter of fact, I did work for her part-time setting appointment for the girls. That's all," Madeline replied.

"You better not be lying to me, because I am going to visit Miss Holly tomorrow and find out the truth," Hunter said in a loud voice.

"That's not necessary. Why don't you trust me, darling? I wouldn't do anything to hurt you," Madeline said.

"I am leaving until this matter is cleared up," Hunter said, slamming the door behind him.

The next morning Hunter paid a visit to Miss Holly. The truth came out; Madeline had been sleeping with everyone in town. Hunter had not only been lied to, but he was disgusted and was badly hurt as well. His life had been shattered by his life's dream, now gone. There was only one thing left to do, and that was to confront Madeline and call off the wedding.

"Madeline you have made a laughingstock out of us. It appears that you have slept with half the town. How could you do this to me? I really thought you loved me and wanted to be my wife," Hunter said with tears in his eyes.

"Please don't go. You can't believe all those lies," Madeline said.

"Unfortunately, the whole town isn't lying. There is nothing left between us." Hunter grabbed his suitcase and turned toward the door. Madeline came screaming behind him, begging him not to leave. After realizing all was lost, she picked up a knife lying on the table and stabbed Hunter several times. He fell over dead on the floor in a pool of blood.

Madeline dropped to her knees over Hunter and thought to herself, *If I couldn't have him no one else could either.*

The next day Madeline reported to the marshal that Hunter had been killed. Madeline tried to pass off the murder by someone on the outside. Following an investigation, it was determined Madeline had bought the knife two days before at the mercantile and had stabbed Hunter to death. Madeline was found guilty of first degree murder, and she became the first female to be hanged in the Wyoming Territory.

MISSEY BLUE

The Civil War was over, with the issue of slavery ending. The plantation owners were trying to hold on to their plantations, but it was not easy with the loss of all their slaves. They had no one to work the fields. Some of the owners were just walking away with whatever they could take with them. The carpetbaggers began to move in and buy up land for as little as $25.00 by just paying the taxes. The cotton and other crops were withering in the field with no one to pick them.

There was a particular plantation owner by the name of Harrison Lawrence who had one young slave girl still in his keeping. Her name was Missey; she was his and one of his slave's daughter. Missey was a beautiful young woman with blue deep set eyes and a tightly braided black ponytail falling down her back. Her skin took on more white than black characteristics. Missey had been well schooled with other white children of her age. Harrison told her he was taking her to a local orphanage, where she would be cared for until she was old enough to be on her own. Missey was only fourteen years old, and she began to cry.

"Please don't cry, Missey. You know I love you as much as I did your mother before she passed away. I don't know where I will end up, and I have no means of taking care for you," Harrison said with a saddened voice.

"Don't send me to the orphanage. I will die there, "Missey said.

"Missey, I don't have any choice. Let's get your belongings together, and I will take you to the orphanage this afternoon. Everything will be all right. You know I will miss you very much, and I will come back for you as soon as I get settled," Harrison said.

Somehow Missey knew she would never see her father again. It was late afternoon as Harrison and Missey pulled up in front of the circular entryway to the orphanage. Harrison helped Missey down and told her to go inside, and they were waiting for her.

"I will be along directly. I will bring your belongings," Harrison told her.

Missey had never been away from the plantation and was trembling with fear. Missey ran back to Harrison standing by the wagon.

"I am afraid to go inside. I have never done anything like this before!" Missey cried.

"Young lady, that's enough of this. You are going to go inside and meet the nice people who will be caring for you. I don't want you to make a scene. Do you understand?" Harrison grabbed Missey by the hand and took her up the wooden steps then knocked on the massive double doors. Someone inside slowly opened the doors to greet Missey and Harrison.

"I am Harrison Lawrence, and I am here to drop off my daughter, Missey. I made arrangements with Miss Angela Scroggins."

About that time a portly middle-aged woman with unruly looking hair walked up behind the servant and introduced herself.

"You must be Harrison, and this is Missey, I presume? I am Angela Scroggins, and I will be watching after your daughter, Mr. Harrison." Missey still had reservations about being at the orphanage, and she refused to shake Angela's hand.

"Missey, don't be rude, Miss Scroggins is very nice, and you need to show some respect!" Harrison said in a stern voice.

Reluctantly Missey extended her right hand with her face turned away.

Miss Scroggins said, "Now that is better, dear. Let me show you to your room."

Missey turned to her father and gave him a hug and kiss. "I will miss you, Father, and I will always think of you."

Harrison gave Missey a kiss and said, "Missey, I will return for you. It won't be that long." He turned and walked away down the steps and to his carriage, and drove off.

From that moment on Missey had no idea what the future would bring. The next morning, all the children went downstairs into a large kitchen with a long hand-hewn table that held twelve places to seat everyone. Missey sat at one end of the table, waiting for the others to take their places.

No sooner had she sat down than she heard a shout from Miss Scroggins, "Missey! Who told you that you could sit at the end of the table?"

"No one. I thought I could sit anywhere I wanted. The other children just took whatever seat they wanted," Missey said.

Miss Scroggins walked over and grabbed Missey by her hair and yanked her out of her seat. "You don't ever sit—and I repeat—sit wherever you want. You wait until I tell you where to sit!"

Missey began to cry and said, "I am sorry! I didn't know I should wait for your permission!"

"That's quite enough, Missey. You may be excused and go directly to your room.

Missey spoke up, "But I didn't get to eat!"

"Maybe next time you will pay closer attention. We have rules around here, and they are not to be broken!" Miss Scroggins shouted in a demeaning voice.

Later that evening Missey heard a knock on her door. Miss Scroggins was extremely jealous of Missey. She was not only pretty but was also well spoken, especially for the time.

When she opened the door a large aging man with short grey hair spoke up, "I am the headmaster. My name is Herbert Strattmore, and I would like you to join me in my quarter. I would like to know more about you." He took Missey by the hand and walked her down the long hallway and to an open end of the orphanage where you could look out over the southern countryside.

"Here, Missey, please sit down by me over here," he said as he pointed to a small settee.

Missey did as she was instructed. Through the conversation Herbert kept sliding closer to Missey, and he began to stroke her hair and face. She immediately jumped to her feet and ran toward the door.

Herbert cut her off before she could reach the door and said, "Missey, if you don't cooperate your punishment could be severe. It's all right this time, but you better never run from me again!" Herbert shouted.

From that day on Missey couldn't seem to do anything right, and she was continually punished for rules that she had never heard of. Two years passed, and there was no sign of Harrison. Missey knew he would never be back for her; if she was to survive the torment of the orphanage, she would have to harden her heart in order to deal with the abuse from Miss Scroggins and the headmaster. Missey worked harder on her homework and other assigned chores than anyone else in the orphanage. It didn't matter—she was punished more than anyone else for things that were minuscule.

One day Herbert came to get Missey, and he took her to his quarters. Missey obeyed and walked with Herbert to the large open room.

"You know, Missey, you are a beautiful woman. You don't look like any of the other girls hear. If you treat me with respect I will give you privileges that none of the others have."

Missey spoke up, "What do you mean by respect? What do I have to do?"

"Oh, I just want you to stay close to me and come down to my quarters whenever I summon you. I believe you will find me to be a generous man in exchange for certain services, that's all," Herbert said.

Missey knew what Herbert had in mind, and she didn't want any part of his scheme. She did everything to avoid him or to be busy with other chores each time he requested her company. Late one night Herbert walked into Missy's room and dragged her out of bed.

"What are you doing? Missey asked?

"You'll see soon enough," Herbert answered.

Once inside Herbert's room he removed a skeleton key from his pocket and locked the door behind him. Herbert made advances toward Missey, ripping her underclothes off, then he brutally raped her. Once he was done he dragged her through the door and left her on the floor crying and bleeding.

Missey crawled down the long hall to her room. She had made up her mind that nothing like this would ever happen again. The next morning Missey joined the others for breakfast with bruises over most of her body. One of the girls asked what happened. Before Missey could say anything Miss Scroggins spoke up, "Missey had an accident last night. Don't worry, she will be all right."

From that day on the girls called her Missey Blue after her black and blue body. After Missey was feeling better, Herbert invited her down to his room.

Missey refused, "You are not going to ever rape me again. I will kill myself first."

"We'll see, young lady. You remember what I said! If you did not provide certain services, your punishment would be severe. I'll ask you one last time. Are you coming with me or not?" Herbert shouted,

Missey replied, "No!"

Herbert shouted for Miss Scroggins to come immediately.

After she arrived Herbert said, "I want you to take her to the root cellar out back and lock her in."

"But Mr. Strattmore, she could die there, with no food or water," Miss Scroggins said.

"Don't argue with me. Just do as I say! That is all. You are dismissed!"

Miss Scroggins grabbed Missey by the arm and forced her to come along. They both went downstairs and out the back of the orphanage to a place covered by large shade tree. Near the base of one of the trees was a root cellar with two large wooden doors meeting in the middle.

"Come here, Missey, and don't you dare run off," Miss Scroggins said while holding on to Missey with one arm and pulling open the two wood doors with the other. The doors were open; Miss Scroggins pushed Missey down the steps headfirst where she landed on a slimy dirt floor.

Missey screamed, "Please don't leave me here! I will die!"

Without a word Miss Scroggins latched the doors together and walked away. One of the other girls overheard where they had taken Missey. Once the word got out the children began to talk among themselves; they were horror stricken by what could happen to them, especially after what happened to Missey.

Miss Scroggins entered the room and heard the children talking about Missey. "Hush, I don't want you talking about Missey, or you will end up the same way."

Two days passed, and Missey was still in the root cellar; she was growing weaker by the day without water or anything to eat. Even Miss Scroggins became concerned and asked Herbert if she could let Missey out.

He answered, "No. She needs to learn her lesson."

By now Missey had grown so weak she couldn't talk. If someone didn't let her up she would die there, and no one would ever know what happened. The end of the third day one of the girls decided to take a chance and let Missey out. She knew if she didn't, Missey would probably die.

Late that night a young black girl named Lucy, who was about Missey's age, silently left her room. She worked her way down the rear staircase where she waited for the right time to escape through the back door. It was cold and rainy; she covered her head with a table cloth.

After she made her way to the root cellar she opened the latch and said, "Missey, are you all right? I am here to help you," Lucy said.

There was no response; Missey was too weak to answer. Lucy decided to go down the cellar steps and find Missey. Lucy spotted Missey lying huddled up in a corner.

"Come with me, Missey. I am going to get you out of this terrible place," Lucy said. Lucy helped Missey her feet and pushed her up out of the cold and wet cellar. Lucy helped Missey along as the two left through the trees away from the orphanage.

Hopefully they wouldn't be noticed until morning; by then, they would be safely away from the orphanage. Lucy was familiar with the lay of the land as she had traveled many times through the same area prior to her mother's death.

The next morning Miss Scroggins and Herbert realized that Lucy and Missey had escaped.

Herbert went to the nearest farm about three miles away and brought back some bloodhounds to track down the two girls. Fortunately, Lucy took Missey through a swampy area, leaving the bloodhounds with a dead-end trail into the swamp.

Two days later the two girls made their way to a small dilapidated farmhouse, and they pounded on the door. The woman of the house came to the door and saw the two girls through the curtain. She thought they were runaways until she brought them inside.

"You poor girls. My name is Wilma Saunders. Tell me what happened."

After telling her what happened, the woman was angry, and she wanted to help the girls rebuild their lives. "You know, girls, I lost my husband in the war, and I am sick and tired of abuse and killing," Wilma said.

"I know where the orphanage is, but I never would have believed that anything like this was going on there," Wilma said.

Wilma let the girls stay with her for two weeks. Missey was getting her strength back, and her bruised and abused body began to heal. Lucy was more afraid that she and Missey would be found and taken back to the orphanage. One year later, Lucy and Missey were still thinking back about the orphanage and the suffering they had been put through. It was time to deal with the problem in a very personal way. Missey had an idea of disguising their identities and returning to the orphanage as representatives of the state overseeing the enforcement of regulations regarding orphanages.

Missey said, "We will send official-looking letters to the orphanage introducing ourselves and the date of our expected arrival."

"It sounds like a good idea, but it's risky," Lucy replied.

"Lucy, have you forgotten the pain and how you were treated not that long ago?" Missey asked.

"I suppose you are right. What is your plan?" Lucy asked.

"It is a simple plan. We will kill Miss Scroggins and Herbert! If you are not willing to go with me, I will kill them both myself. Can I count on you or not?" Missey asked.

"But why do we have to kill them?" Lucy asked.

"You may not have a reason, but I do. Thanks to those two, I am unable to bear children. They took from me one of the most precious things in life," Missey said.

"I do understand your feelings, and I am with you all the way," Lucy said.

"We will allow two weeks for the letters to reach the orphanage. Then we will leave," Missey said. "After we arrive I want you to allow me about an hour before you shoot Miss Scroggins. This will allow me enough time to kill Herbert."

Two weeks later they rented a carriage and traveled to the orphanage where they were both greeted by Herbert and Miss Scroggins. Missey introduced herself as Miss Purcell and Lucy as Miss Penelope.

Missey said, "Why don't you have Miss Scroggins show you around, and I will interview Mr. Strattmore." Missey knew that Herbert would be interested in any sexual favors, and it would be easy to lure him in to her plot. Missey asked Herbert to sit down by her on the small settee as they had before. Herbert jumped at the chance. Missey cuddled up closer and pulled up her pantaloons above the knee. Herbert could not resist and placed his hand on her bare knee.

"You know, you are a very handsome man. In fact, you are the type of man I could settle down with," Missey said.

"You are very beautiful yourself, and I would welcome the opportunity to see you again," Herbert said.

"Why we don't get a little more comfortable?" Missey asked as she began taking her clothes off. Herbert wasted no time in removing his trousers and snuggled close to Missey, kissing her all over.

Missey was now sitting on top of Herbert and said, "Don't you remember me," as she pulled off her wig.

"Why, it's you!" Herbert exclaimed.

"Yes, it is me, you bastard. And you are a dead man," Missey said as she pulled out a knife from under her stocking and plunged the blade into Herbert's throat, twisting it around until she knew he was dead. Blood spewed everywhere as his eyes were ready to explode. One gasp, and he was dead. Shortly thereafter Missey heard a gunshot down stairs, killing Miss Scroggins. Missey walked down stairway into the parlor where she saw Miss Scroggins slumped over with a gunshot to the head.

"Well, Lucy, I believe we've wrapped up everything here, don't you think?" Missey asked.

Lucy and Missey walked out the front door, climbed into the carriage, and went back to town.

RIVER OF REDEMPTION

The full moon flooded through the cottonwoods and spread across the river like a quiet phantom. Night had fallen, and the herd was milling around without a sense of tomorrow's river crossing. The outriders were singing to the cattle in a calming voice, preventing them from wandering and becoming restless. The large herd of longhorns was positioned back from the river's edge for the night. The reflection of the campfire shining on the water danced in the night.

The drive had taken the wranglers over eight hundred miles through desolate, hostile, and arid country. The only reason for a man to take on this life-threatening work was for the money or the hope of being able to buy a small spread or a fresh start somewhere.

The Saunders brand was etched into the hide of every animal. Jim Saunders was the owner of the Double Slash ranch in southwestern Texas. The ranch covered more than one hundred square miles. Jim had two sons, one named Clay and the other Ned. The two boys were nothing but trouble, and they were ruthless like their father. Jim had raised his sons in the same manner as a slave owner.

He was only interested in self-gain, even if it meant killing. Regrettably Clay and Ned followed in their father's footsteps. The Saunders had developed a circle of fear around them. Even the men they employed lived in constant fear. Each man knew if anything went wrong he could pay with his life. Yet the charismatic appeal of the Saunders family and the pay kept most men eagerly willing to work in a high stakes inhospitable environment.

The youngest member of the cattle drive was a ten-year-old boy named Mark Cottrell. He was picked up along the way by drovers after his family had been massacred by the Comanche. Mark was found kneeling alongside his mother and sister who had been brutally killed. This was a few weeks back. Mark had responded to the incident with neither tears nor anything vocal. It was possible that he had been traumatized and was too young to understand what happened.

Mark had been assigned to help the cook and maintain the chuck wagon. He had not spoken a word since joining the drive.

The cook was a crusty old cowboy who took a real liking to Mark and tried to teach him everything about preparing meals, along with packing and moving the camp each day.

At the end of the day Mark laid out his bedroll under the chuck wagon and crawled inside with his clothes on. He pulled a rain slicker over his head to keep out the cold.

"See you in the morning, cowboy," the cook said quietly. Mark rolled over on his back and went to sleep while gazing up at the stars from beneath the chuck wagon. The skies had been clear all day with no trace of storm clouds.

The last challenge confronting the men was to get the herd of longhorns across the river before reaching the railhead a few days out. At daybreak Mark heard the cowboys stirring and talking while wrapping their hands around hot cups of coffee to warm them up. With his fists Mark rubbed his eyes, waking himself up and shaking off the tiredness before slowly pulling his weary body out from beneath his bedroll.

The booming voice of Jim Saunders could be heard along the river.

"Okay, boys, get your worthless bodies up! We have a job to do! I'm not paying you to sleep on the job!"

After everyone had been rousted out Jim gathered everyone around.

"Men, I don't expect to lose one head of cattle today. I expect each of you to do your part. Make sure none of the animals drift downstream and keep an eye out for Indians! The river is higher than normal because of the recent rains. You need to keep the herd tight and keep them moving. Otherwise, we could lose a lot of cattle! If anyone loses one head because of slacking on the job, $25.00 will be deducted for each critter lost from your pay at the end of the drive. Now does anyone have any questions?"

There was a long pause. Out of fear, no man dared to raise a question.

"If not, then saddle up and get to work! One last thing, if any man doesn't pull his share I will deal with him personally! All right then, let's get those longhorns across the river."

Mark and the cook would be the last to cross in the chuck wagon.

"Come on, boy. Help me get everything packed up, so we can move out!" the cook yelled.

The wranglers began channeling the cattle to keep them from spreading out. Several hundred head had been driven midway across the river when the wind suddenly flared up, causing the water to heave and cascade. Clouds began to form, growing darker and darker.

Strangeness fell over the river. An hour before, the skies were an azure color with no clouds in sight, beckoning all to a beautiful day. Rain started to fall, escalating into a tempest that was being driven by some unknown force.

The cattle were bawling and drifting downstream because of the swift current. The drovers could not keep the cattle from separating. Thunder rolled across the sky with flashes of lightening piercing the water, striking men and cattle in its path. From the bowels of hell the wrath of Satan had descended upon man and beast. Men yelled as their horses reared, throwing them off in the torrential waters. Jim was yelling threats at some of the riders; they had lost control over the herd.

Some of the wranglers were trying to save their lives by reaching the other side of the river but were pulled under by the undertow created by the storm or shot by the Saunders. The cries of the men and animals could be heard between gunshots and the clap of thunder. The scream of horses caused by the fear of drowning continued until the last one drowned. There was so much panic and confusion that all sense of control was lost. It was a matter of survival with every man attempting to save his own life.

Mark and the cook followed the last head of longhorns into the river. As the chaos continued, the cook motioned for Mark to jump from the chuck wagon and swim back to shore. He knew that the wagon would never make it to the other side of the river.

Stopping momentarily, Mark gazed upon the death and horror before jumping into the churning water. There was no time to look back. The best he could do was reach the river's edge. The force of raging water kept pushing him away from the bank and further out into the river. After several attempts at swimming to shore, Mark grabbed onto a branch from a downed cottonwood tree which was careening over the water. Eventually working his way up the branch, he reached the river's edge. Mark turned to view the death in the river, only to watch the cook holding onto the reins disappear beneath the water while looking back at him.

Mark fell to his knees and cried out loud for the first time since seeing his family massacred. He stood on the shore and watched until the last rider and head of cattle disappeared below the treacherous water.

As suddenly as the storm appeared the wind and rain subsided, and the clouds began to recede. There was no remaining sign of life. The river had yielded up nothing but death to all who tried to cross. Miraculously, Mark was the only thing left living. Mark set down on the river's edge with his head in his hands, brushing away the stain of tears off his cheeks. He looked up to see an occasional horn or piece of tack surface momentarily before disappearing beneath the shadowy water.

The only sound was that of the gentle water pushing its way downstream. The sudden calm had a chilling effect. Mark noticed a change in the river. Before, it was so clear you could watch the fish swimming. The water was now murky, and nothing could be seen in the river.

Mark lay on the bank looking up toward the sun, attempting to unravel the mystery of what had just happened. He was distraught and alone. Not knowing what to do, Mark decided to follow the river until he came to a town. There was no sign of anyone, not even an Indian.

The morning of the second day, Mark continued on until late afternoon. He was so tired he lay down in the shade for a nap. He awoke to the sound of riders approaching. He wasn't sure what to do, so he ran through the trees along the river trying to outrun them. The two men spotted Mark and rode toward him at a full gallop.

As they grew closer, one of them yelled, "Don't be afraid, son! We are not going to hurt you." Mark stopped in his tracks then turned to face the two men who had ridden upon him. They were looking for a place to bed down for the night.

Realizing he was cold and afraid, the men comforted Mark before making camp. The next morning they took Mark to the nearest town, which was about thirty miles to the north. Mark was turned over to the sheriff who later took him to the local orphanage. The only thing anyone knew about Mark was that his parents had been killed by the Comanche. No thought was given to what happened to the men and herd of cattle that disappeared before Mark arrived that ominous day.

Fifteen years passed, and a town was built along the river of carnage.

Stories of what happened years gone by were imagined by people moving into town. Once in a while, someone crossing the river would spot a piece of rotted hide or remnants of a broken hoof turn up in the river then drift downstream. There was a feeling of energy in and around the river crossing with no noticeable sign of what happened.

Mark had studied for the ministry and had become a preacher. He had decided to move to the new town being built along the river, where he had barely escaped death many years before as a young boy. As the preacher, he was asked to become a member of the newly formed town council where a name for the new town was to be decided upon. In the course of the evening several names were discussed; however, no one could agree on any of them.

Mark listened intently to the disagreement among the men before speaking up.

"I have a suggestion. Having been here before, I have an appropriate name for our new town. The name that I have chosen is Redemption."

"What kind of a name is that?" one of the other men yelled.

"Let me explain my reason for the name," the preacher replied.

Another man spoke up. "Preacher, what do you know about what happened here?"

"Before we continue let me answer all of your questions. I was here that dreadful day and was the only one that survived." After explaining how he became a part of the cattle drive and his job working with the cook, Mark explained what he witnessed on the day of holocaust many years before. While listening to Mark, there was stony silence in the room as he covered every meticulous detail.

One of the men asked, "Why do you think such a terrible thing like that happened?"

"I believe it was the Lord's retribution for how Jim Saunders and his men lived their lives. Jim Saunders and his sons were known killers, doing anything necessary to acquire more land and cattle. Everyone was punished for the evil that each man did. It reminded me of Sodom and Gomorrah. There was so much wickedness that the Lord had no choice but to destroy everything living as part of the Saunders's legacy."

For some the mystery was over, leaving others with a labyrinth of unanswered questions.

THE DEVIL'S RIM

The sky quickly faded to black with clouds building in the south. The stage was due in Arroyo before nightfall. Frank Pivens was riding shotgun, and Joe Fargo was the driver.

"It looks like rain ahead. Maybe we should stop and put our ponchos on," Joe said. Frank pointed to a wide spot in the road where they could stop.

"Yaw, this looks like a good place. I will let the passengers know why we are stopping!" Joe yelled. Joe brought the team to a slow stop then jumped down from his seat.

"Well, folks, it looks like it is going to rain up ahead. We're just putting on our gear in case. If it starts raining hard you might want to pull the window shades down. Oh, another thing. Everyone needs to stay in their seat and not move around because once we reach the summit, we will be going down a steep narrow area of the trail overlooking a cliff to the right. There's no need to worry. Frank and I have driven this stretch for years and have never had any problems. You might want to get out and stretch your bones a little though." After everyone was back on the stage, Joe and Frank climbed back on top ready to go.

Joe grabbed the reins and yelled, "Come on you, lazy critters, let's get movin'!"

He cracked the whip above the lead horse, and they lunged forward, pulling the coach behind them. The sky was black, and the rain started to fall. Joe slowed the team down as the trail was getting slicker. Suddenly a lightning bolt pierced the sky, followed by a clap of thunder. The horses were beginning to spook and were starting to twist in their harnesses.

"Whoa! Take it easy, boys, there is no need to panic," Joe said in a controlled voice. The horses settled down, but the sound of thunder kept them uneasy. The rain started to fall as if someone had opened up the clouds and emptied them on everyone. The stage had reached the summit and was now headed downhill. It was approaching the narrow part of the trail where the cliff on the right side drops several hundred feet below into the canyon.

"Frank, I need your help with the brake! I can't hold the team and the brake too! We are starting to slide!" Joe shouted.

Several shots rang out, causing the horses to bolt. Joe turned to say something to Frank, but he was gone. One of the passengers pulled back the shade on his side; he could make out several riders through the blinding rain. The stage was picking up momentum as it continued down the mountain side. With Frank gone Joe knew he was in trouble.

Joe yelled at the top of his voice, "Whoa! You crazy critters!" but the horses were spooked, and they never broke stride.

The trail was slicker now, and the coach began sliding from side to side, approaching the rim. The team was out of control, and the stage was veering closer to the edge. More gunshots rang out, causing the horses to run harder. The visibility was so poor that Joe could barely see the rim's edge coming up on the right side. The stage was coming into a long left turn as the wheels on the outside were spinning in the air. Suddenly one of the lead horses lost its footing, falling down on his knees and dragging down the other horses, causing the stage to roll on its side before going over the rim.

Screams could be heard from the passengers inside. One woman grabbed her little girl holding a small teddy bear; she pulled the little girl to her breast, covering her eyes so that she could not witness her fate. The horses gave out a diabolical shrill that had never been heard before as they plummeted to the canyon floor below.

Along the cliff face to the valley floor below lay mutilated bodies and dead horses everywhere. Pieces of human and horse flesh along with tack were visible on the rocks and in the trees. It appeared as if the Devil himself had strewn the stage along with everything else against the side of the cliff, waiting to see it fall to the canyon below.

One of the wheels came lose, and a passenger thrown from the stage landed on a splintered piece of a spoke which pierced his chest and killed him instantly. The storm grew into a maelstrom as the night progressed.

The stage was overdue by four hours. People were milling around the street waiting for the stage. They were nervous and upset, especially those waiting for family and friends. People were beginning to line up at the stage office to find out what was going on.

Will Higgins, who managed the stage office, told everyone that he didn't know anything; they knew as much as he did.

"As soon as the weather breaks we will form a posse and look for the stage. We can't go out in this weather until the storm slows down."

By now Tom Rankin, the sheriff, saw all the people in front of the stage office and walked across the street to find out why all the commotion.

"Tom, I told everyone that we couldn't go out in this weather and find anything. Tomorrow if the weather breaks we will take a posse and search for the stage," Will said.

"That makes the most sense, folks! I know you are all concerned, the same as we are. I promise you that we'll do everything possible as soon as we can to find out what happened. Meanwhile, everyone needs to leave and get some rest. Tomorrow we have a long day ahead," Tom said.

The next morning at sunup, a posse along with an Apache tracker set out looking for the wayward stage and passengers.

"Let's stay close together in single file up the mountain," Will told everyone.

As the riders reached the summit there was no sign of the stage. The tracker rode ahead but could find no tracks of any kind. Suddenly he came upon a body lying face down in the mud. He motioned for everyone to come. One of the riders stopped, walked over to the dead man, then rolled him over to see who he was.

"Look, it's Frank Pivens! My god, the back of his head is gone," Will said. One of the riders saw something further up the trail, something shining on the ground. He slid off his horse and walked over to the object.

"Look, it is silver concho from a belt or a vest. I'll bring it along."

Apparently everything else had been washed away by the storm, including any wagon wheel ruts.

"This is mighty strange if you ask me. How could a stage with six people and a full team of horses just disappear?" the sheriff asked.

"Something terrible happened last night, and we'll get to the bottom of it if it's the last thing we do," Will said.

The riders had ridden up and down the mountain five miles in both directions with no sign of the stage or passengers.

"In the morning we will split up. I'll take four men and the Indian, and we'll scour Saguaro Canyon while the rest of you continue searching up here where the concho was found. We aren't going back without finding the stage. If anyone runs across anything, fire two shots," the sheriff remarked.

"Okay, Tom, that sounds like a good idea. Hopefully we will turn up something. Meanwhile, let's turn in. We could have a rough day ahead," replied Will.

At sunup, Tom and the four other men along with the Indian tracker started the long decent down the mountain into the canyon below. The day was hot, and the horses needed water. There was a small stream at the bottom of the canyon where they stopped and watered the horses and cooled off. The tracker slowly worked his way up the valley, looking for any sign of the stage. About half an hour later the four men caught up with the scout. The Indian slowly crossed another stream then stopped his pony and slid down. There was some kind of debris floating in the water. He motioned for Tom and the others.

The tracker pointed toward the water. "Look, it is white man's clothing!"

Tom jumped down from his horse and looked at the piece of clothing. It was a piece of a woman's dress that had drifted into a stand of willows.

"This must be from one of the passengers. It is a clean garment that was torn off. We need to move up the valley. We must be getting closer to either the stage or what happened!" Will explained.

The tracker motioned for everyone to spread out as they rode up the canyon. It wasn't too long after riding up a narrow draw that the horror of what happened unfolded before their eyes. Tom pulled out his revolver and fired two shots. As the others approached, the remains and the horses flesh were already starting to decompose in the heat of the day. Each rider placed a kerchief over his face to ward off the stench. This was the most gruesome spectacle that anyone had ever witnessed. By now Will and the others had made their way down the mountain into the canyon.

Tom turned to Will and said, "You need to cover your mouth. You may not want to look at what's happened here. This is the worst tragedy I have ever seen. We need to check for any sign of life first and then get what's left of the bodies out of the sun. Look in the sky. The buzzards have already spotted the dead and are circling overhead, just waiting for us to leave."

"Meanwhile someone needs to go back to town and bring a couple of wagons so that we can at least carry the dead back for burial," Will suggested.

"Why don't you and Fred go back to town for the wagons, and we'll look for anyone that may still be alive?" Tom asked.

Everyone spread out, checking each body for any sign of life. Two men had to scale the cliff side to check a body that was hanging off a rock. The only thing left of the coach was one rear seat attached to one side of the stage. Everything else looked like kindling wood. The horses were all dead and badly mutilated. Tom walked over to one of the dead horses and saw a man pinned underneath.

"Come over here!" Tom yelled. "There's a man pinned under this horse, and I need help in pulling him out. I think he is still alive."

One of the men helping the sheriff recognized the man after slowly rolling the horse over far enough to free him. The sheriff laid his head next to the man's chest to see if he was breathing.

"Do you know who this is?" one of the men asked.

"No, who is he?" Tom replied.

"That is Lee Hollis, a United States Marshal out of Kansas. I met him years ago in Abilene. He was a fine man and had the fastest draw I have ever seen."

"Hand me a canteen. This man is still breathing. He is trying to say something but is too weak to talk. Marshal, don't try to talk. We have sent for help. We are taking you back to Arroyo as soon as we have a wagon. He appears to be the only survivor. Make sure he is as comfortable as possible and get him out of the sun."

Two hours passed, and there was still no sign of the wagons. The sky was clouding over, and the rain had started again.

"We need to get what's left of these bodies out of the rain and away from the wild animals!" Tom yelled.

Three men began picking up the remains and dragging them under the cactus and the trees. Including Lee Hollis, there was a man along with a young woman and small child. Three hours went by before any sign of the wagons arriving. The rain started to pick up.

"Place your rain slickers over those bodies!" Tom yelled.

Through the blowing rain one of the men could make out a wagon coming toward them.

"We brought two wagons!" one of the drivers yelled.

"Bring the wagons over here, closer to the tree. The marshal is over here, and we need to get him in the wagon!" Tom said. After laying two blankets out in the bottom of the wagon, three men picked up the marshal and laid him in the buckboard then covered him with a poncho.

"I don't know if we should load up the other bodies, or should we just bury them here?" someone said.

Tom decided to take the bodies back to Arroyo for identification. On the way back the sun came out, and the bodies began to heat up and throw off a stench.

"Get some wet blankets over those bodies. It will help them from decomposing faster," Will said.

The return trip was slow and arduous as the marshal was still alive, and they wanted to keep him that way. After arriving back in town they took the marshal over to the doctor. They took him inside and laid him out on a table. The marshal slowly turned his head and beckoned for someone to come closer so that he could tell them something.

The marshal whispered, "I don't think it is a good idea to let anyone know that I am still alive. This whole situation could be because of me. I just don't know."

After discussing the matter it was agreed that when this came out in the newspaper it would state everyone died in the accident.

Will said, "Where can we take the marshal? He is going to need a lot of care until he gets back on his feet."

"Millie Hays, who owns the roadhouse, is a close friend of the Marshal. And she was with him when his wife had passed away. Maybe she will be willing to take him in and care for him until he ready to leave."

Will explained to Millie what happened and without a word, she rushed through the back door across the street to the doctor's office to find Lee. Millie looked down at Will and began to cry. He was not only a good friend but was also always there for her. Lee had a gentle side that very few people saw.

"Lee sent a telegram last month saying he wanted to come see me and spend a few days to get away and relax. I just figured he wasn't coming, and I was getting concerned," Millie replied.

Late that night four men carried the marshal to Millie's place. Several days later the marshal asked to see the concho.

After carefully inspecting it he said, "This looks like a concho from a Mexican tapadero. It's larger than a regular belt concho."

"Where would something like this come from?" Tom asked.

The marshal replied, "It is probably off a Mexican saddle from someone either living in Mexico or somewhere on the boarder. I can't say for sure, but I think I have seen a concho like this before. I just can't place where," the marshal replied.

Four months had passed, and the marshal had gotten most of his strength back—except for the use of his right hand, which had been crushed in the accident. He knew he would have to learn to draw and shoot with his left hand, or he would never be able to shoot again.

One night he told Millie he was going to leave, but he would be back in a few days, there's no reason to worry.

"At least tell me where you are going! You are not well enough to be out on your own yet," Millie explained out of concern.

"I am going to practice my draw using my left hand. I will be just fine," Lee replied.

After three days Lee Hollis rode back into town late at night. Lee became comfortable with the use of his left hand over the next two months. After returning to town one night, he told Millie he was going to leave the next night and that he might not come back.

"I have to find out who drove the stage over the rim and killed all those innocent people, or I will never find peace again."

Around a corner across from the boarding house stood a man in the shadows, listening to the conversation between the marshal and Millie. He quietly stepped back on the boardwalk and then ran down the street. He jumped on a horse and galloped off. The man rode all night until he reached the small border town of Nacho. After catching his breath he ran into the saloon, where he spotted two men standing at the bar.

He approached the two me at the bar and said, "You need to listen to me. Lee Hollis is still alive."

One of the men turned and said, "Zach, I think you've lost your mind. Lee Hollis died in that stage accident along with everyone else. Everyone knows that. What the hell is wrong with you, anyway?"

"No, you're wrong. Lee Hollis is not dead. I saw him early last night and overheard him telling a woman that he was leaving town and probably would not be back. He said he had to find out who caused the stage accident, or he would never find peace again."

"Are you sure it was Hollis and not someone who looked like him?"

"What do you think, Pike? Do you think he knows we were involved?"

"Well, if he doesn't, he will figure it out. It's just a matter of time," Rans said.

"Let's get back to the ranch and talk things over and decide what to do," Pike remarked. If you hear of anything about the marshal coming our way, you need to let me know! Have you got that, boy?" Pike snarled.

The young man left town in a hurry, and the other two men left town in the opposite direction. The marshal knew he had to be careful in Nacho while he was looking for the men he thought had run the stage off the mountain. The first thing he had to do was find out who the rider was who lost the concho; this could lead him to the killers.

Back at the ranch, the three men discussed their plan to kill the marshal if he came after them, especially after having killed their brother in Wichita.

"Rans, I think you should ride into town tomorrow and look around for any sign of the marshal. The two of you have never met. He won't suspect anything. If you aren't back by noon we will come looking for you," Pike said.

Lee Hollis mounted up and rode to Nacho. He knew the man he had killed in a gunfight two years before in Wichita was one of the notorious Pfarro brothers. The others may have gotten word somehow that he was on the stage to Arroyo and sacrificed all the passengers to kill him. It was only a hunch; he would have to track these killers down wherever they were.

Early that morning the marshal rode up to the only saloon in Nacho. After climbing down from his horse and dusting himself off, he noticed a horse tied to the hitching post with tapaderos covering the stirrups. He walked around the horse to the other side and checked the tapadero. One of the tapederos was missing something. He reached inside his vest pocket and pulled out the silver concho, placing it on the tapadero where the piece was missing. It was the same design as the other side. Lee knew whoever rode this horse must be one of the killers. He walked up the stairs and threw open the saloon doors and looked for anyone suspicious.

The marshal shouted, "Who does that Appaloosa belong to?"

A man standing at the bar said, "It's my horse, and what's it to you?" he barked.

"What is your name, mister? Because if that's your horse, you are under arrest for murder!" the marshal shouted.

"Just who do you think you are, and besides, no one is going to arrest me for anything!" the man said in a loud voice.

"I am a US Marshal. My name is Lee Hollis, and I am looking for the men who ran a stagecoach off the rim, killing five people above Saguaro Canyon last year."

The man replied, "What does this have to do with me, Marshal?"

The marshal reached into his vest pocket and pulled out the silver concho.

"Have you ever seen this before?"

"No, I can't say that I have," replied the man.

"That's strange. I looked at the tapaderos on your horse, and this concho matches the one that was missing from one of your stirrups," the marshal said. "This was found on the rim above Saguaro canyon the day after the stage incident! This belongs to you, and I am charging you with murder! Now, we can do this one of two ways. You can either drop your gun belt or draw. I swear I will kill you where you stand!"

The man backed up, ready to draw.

"I want to know something else. Who else was involved in these killings? You must be one of the Pfarro brothers," the marshal asked.

"You're right, Marshal. And you know what? My brothers will be looking for you."

"I am curious to know how you knew I was on that stage."

"It was easy, Marshal. When my brothers and I rode into Wichita after you killed our brother, I happened to run into another man who hated your guts as well. He told me you had his father hanged for a bank robbery he wasn't in on. He was willing to keep an eye on you and let us know if you ever planned on coming this way."

"So you and the likes of your family trash decided to murder everyone on the stage to get to me!" the marshal shouted.

"That pretty well sums it up all right, Marshal."

Before another word was spoken the man drew his gun, but he was shot before his gun cleared the holster. The man lay dead on the saloon floor. The bar tender piped up, "You know, Marshal, you're going to have to deal with the Pfarro brothers alone in this town. No one will help! Everyone's afraid to get involved. They have a small spread just on the other side of the border. That way they can rob and murder on the American side and then escape back across the border."

"How far is their spread from Nacho?" the marshal asked.

"About five miles straight south of here," replied the bartender.

Without saying a word, the marshal dragged the body feet first from the saloon down the steps to the ground. It started to rain as the marshal continued to drag the body over to the horse; he wrapped one leg to the stirrup then took the silver concho from his pocket, and he stuffed it in the dead man's mouth. He then removed his scarf and tied it around his head to keep the concho from falling out.

The marshal drew his revolver and fired two shot in to the air. The horse bolted and headed south through the rain, heading back to the spread across the border where the two men were waiting. Lee knew that if the horse made its way back to the two brothers, they would come back to kill him. The marshal led his horse down the muddy street to the livery stable and asked the liveryman if he could leave his horse there for a while. The man told him he could but asked when he would be back.

The marshal replied, "I don't know. But if I don't come back, the horse and saddle are yours. You can do whatever you want to do with them."

The rain finally eased up, and the sun begun to appear through the clouds. It was late morning, and now the marshal could only wait.

In the middle of town was a plaza and a public well, surrounded on all side by an adobe wall. You could see anyone coming from all directions. This is where the marshal decided to wait for the other two killers. It was about noon when he looked over the adobe wall and saw two riders slowly coming in. One of them turned, riding behind one of the dilapidated adobe buildings, which were the remains of an old church. The other man stopped in front of the saloon then went inside. Within minutes the man coming out of the saloon yelling, "Marshal, you son of a bitch! Come out where I can see you, or don't you have the guts? This is between you and me! You have just killed the last Pfarro!"

"Where is your brother? I saw him ride into town with you. What are you planning to do—shoot me in the back like your brother in Wichita did to that poor man who was drunk and unarmed?"

Out of the corner of his eye, the marshal caught sight of a man standing on top of the adobe church; he was holding on to the spire with one hand and a rifle in the other pointed at the marshal, ready to shoot when he stood up. By now the other brother was standing in front, facing the plaza.

After careful thought the marshal rolled to the opposite side to where the brother with the rifle was waiting and shot the man twice. In an attempt to hang on to the belfry rope he lost his balance, falling in to the watering trough in front of the old church. The other brother shot the marshal in the right shoulder after rolling out from behind the adobe wall. Not realizing the marshal had learned to shoot with his other hand, the marshal shot him in the chest. He dropped to his knees then fell to the ground.

Both men were dead, but the marshal had taken a bullet tearing through his shoulder, leaving a gaping hole on the back side. He was beginning to bleed. He knew he needed help, but with no doctor or anyone else around to help, he would have to try to make it out of town on his own. He staggered back toward the livery stable to get his horse. By now the blood was streaming down his chest and shoulder; he was growing weaker. After a couple more steps he collapsed, falling over dead on the street. The people watching what had happened just walked by and looked down on the body without saying a word. It was not their concern!

THE STRANGER

"This is the last thing we need. Another drifter in our town!" one of the men shouted. The two men sitting on the boardwalk watched as the rider approached them.

"Stranger, where ya from?" asked the other man. The stranger said nothing and rode on down the street, pulling his horse up in front of the saloon. He was a man of large stature with a rugged-looking face buried behind a shaggy beard, with piercing dark blue eyes, and unkept coal black hair. His shoulders were broad, which became immediately noticeable as he slowly climbed down from his horse, shaking his hat and trail coat from the dust. After tying his horse up he walked through the saloon doors, leaving them swinging behind him as he walked up to the bar.

"What will ya have, mister?" the bartender barked.

"Just something cold," he replied.

"Hell, that could be anything from sarsaparilla to milk," yelled the bartender before laughing out loud.

"In case you didn't know, this is a bar where liquor is served," a man standing at the bar said.

The stranger turned to the man and gave him a look as if he was staring through his soul, then turned to the man and said, "You could use some manners, mister."

The man reached for his gun, but before he could draw, the stranger effortlessly picked him up and placed the man on the bar before sending him on his way like a bottle of beer. He landed on a poker table and crashed to the floor. The four men around the table saw what was happening and jumped out of the way. Without saying a word the stranger walked out of the saloon.

After picking himself up off the broken table the man said, "No one treats me like that and gets away with it. The next time I see him I'm going to kill him!"

"What were you going to do, Mert, shoot an unarmed man?"

"Oh, shut up, Henry!"

The stranger walked across the street to the hotel where he inquired about a room and bath. The desk clerk told him it would be one dollar a night for the room and fifty cents for the bath then asked him how long he planned on staying.

"I don't know," he said, placing a gold nugget on the counter, "this should take care of it for a few days, don't you think?"

"Why, yes, sir. Please sign in right here," the desk clerk replied while handing the stranger the key. "Your room is at the top of the stairs, second on the right, number 205."

After the stranger walked upstairs carrying his saddlebags, the desk man turned the registration book around to read the stranger's name.

"Mitch Rankin," the desk clerk repeated under his breath. "That's a real different name."

A short time later, the stranger came back down the stairs and asked where he could board his horse.

"The livery stable is down the street, past the newspaper office on the same side."

Mitch walked outside and led his horse down the street to the livery stable. There was no one in sight.

"Anybody here?" he yelled.

"Be right there!" a man replied. "What can I do for you, mister?"

"I need to board my horse for a few days. What do you charge?"

"It will cost you fifty cents a day, plus another twenty-five cents for hay and thirty-five cents for oats, which ever you prefer."

"Here's five dollars to get started. I want you to give him a good rubdown and oats every other day," the stranger replied.

"Yes, sir. If I need to reach you, where will you be staying?" the liveryman asked.

"I'm staying up the street at the Henley House," he replied as he turned and walked away.

The next morning Mitch walked down the street to the livery stable to get his horse.

The liveryman approached him and asked, "I don't know if you're interested or not, mister, but are you—by chance—looking for a job?"

"As a matter of fact, I am!" the stranger replied.

"After you left here last night, I remembered that a widow who lost her husband in the war was looking for someone to help out around her place. It's run-down and needs a lot of work. Her name is Margaret Collins. Everyone calls her Maggie. She lives about five miles west of town, off the old stage road. Just stay to the left, and you will ride right to her small spread. There is something you need to know about Maggie. She is quite religious, and she has a young son. Oh, I didn't catch your name?"

"My name is Rankin—Mitch Rankin—and thanks for the information."

Mitch mounted up and galloped off. Following the road to the left he started to make out several small run-down buildings.

This must be Maggie's place. How could anyone live out here under these conditions? Mitch thought.

He climbed down from his horse and was about to tie it up when he heard someone yell, "What are you doing here, mister?" Mitch looked up to see a double barrel shotgun pointed at him.

"Mom, are you going to shoot him?" a small boy asked.

"No, Trace, I'm not going to shoot him unless I have to," the woman replied.

"Ma'am, are you Mrs. Collins?"

"Well, what if I am? And who are you?" the woman said in a stern voice.

"Then you are the person I need to talk to, ma'am. My name is Mitch. The man running the livery stable gave me your name and said you might be looking for help."

"Mister, as you can see, this place is so run-down I don't have much hope of ever getting it back to what it was before the war. The other problem is that I can't afford to pay anyone."

"I am sorry for the difficult time you must be having, especially since losing your husband."

"What do you know about my husband? You know nothing about him or the kind of man he was. He was strong, supportive, and god-fearing as any man could be. The war took him from me. He was killed in Vicksburg, leaving me with a son to raise in this hellhole of a place."

"Ma'am, I don't doubt what you're saying at all. I didn't come out here to talk about your husband. I am just asking for a job."

"I am sorry, it has been so long since I met a real gentleman. And I suppose I have forgotten my manners. My name is Margaret, but you can call me Maggie. This is my son, Trace. He just turned seven."

Mitch reached out to shake Trace's hand, but he turned to his mother, burying his head in her apron.

"Trace, you can at least be nice to the man!"

"No offense taken, ma'am. It's nice meeting both of you. Just call me Mitch. I just need work, that's all. My needs are minimal. I mainly need a place to bed down. I am willing to work for room and board and whatever you can afford to pay. Is that fair enough?"

"I suppose so. Just don't expect much, and neither of us will be disappointed."

"I'll put my belongings in the barn. That's where I will sleep, if that's all right."

"I am sorry, I don't have a bunkhouse for you to sleep in. At least you can eat in the house with us," Maggie responded.

The next morning Maggie said to Mitch, "Before anything else happens, you need a haircut and shave. I want to see the man underneath all that hair."

After cutting his hair and giving Mitch a good shave, Maggie turned to Trace and said under her breath, "He's not half bad looking for a man."

"Thank you for the haircut and shave, ma'am."

"And another thing. Please stop calling me ma'am. I want you to call me Maggie from now on."

One morning Mitch told Maggie he needed to go to town to pick up some barbed wire and fence post to replace the section of fence behind the barn.

"Go to the Valley Mercantile and ask for Ed Larson. I have an account with him, but I'm not sure whether he will give me any more credit since I still owe him from a couple of years back."

"Well, there's only one way to find out. I'll take the buckboard. I should be back by supper," Mitch said.

"Be careful, and we'll see you tonight," Maggie replied.

After hooking up the team Mitch headed out. After reaching town, Mitch pulled up in front of the mercantile, jumped down from wagon, and then walked inside. "I'm looking for Ed Larson."

"I'm Ed Larson. What can I do for you?"

"My name is Mitch. I work for Mrs. Collins, and she asked me to pick up some supplies."

"What do you need young man?"

"I need twenty-five posts, two rolls of barbed wire, and a couple sacks of grain."

"You know, Mrs. Collins owes me quite a lot of money. Let me see how much. I'm not sure I can extend her any more credit right now."

"Mr. Larson, if I may ask, exactly how much does she owe?"

"Well, let's see. With this order and everything else, the total will be $185.00."

"What if I payoff Maggie's account: would that help?"

"Why, sure. But you don't have to do that, mister," Ed replied.

Mitch laid out three hundred dollars on the counter and told Ed to use the balance for the future.

"There is one thing, though. I don't want Maggie to know about this!"

"Okay, let me help you load up. The posts and wire are back in the store room," Ed replied.

All the items were loaded up except for the grain. Mitch walked out of the store with a sack of grain on each shoulder when a man stepped between him and the wagon.

"What can I do for you, mister?" Mitch asked.

"I told you the next time I saw you I would kill you. Don't you remember from the other day?"

"Yes, I remember your loud mouth, if that's what you are asking. Do you always pick a bad time to kill someone? Can't you see I'm busy?"

A shot rang out; the man shot a hole in one of grain sacks. The grain started to fall out over Mitch's shoulder on the ground. Mitch threw the other sack on the ground. "Well, mister, if you are going to kill me you had better get on with it, or leave me alone."

The man backed up and said, "Someone throw him a gun, or I swear I will shoot him where he stands."

A man standing in front of the mercantile threw Mitch a gun.

Mitch placed the gun in his belt and said, "You know, mister, you don't have to die."

"For a man who doesn't carry a gun you are pretty damned sure of yourself," the man replied. The man backed up a little more and said, "When I count to three, draw!"

Mitch's eyes locked on his, waiting for the man to draw. The man started to reach for his gun; with blinding speed Mitch drew the gun from his belt and shot the man before his gun had cleared the holster. The man fell to the ground with a look of astonishment on his face then slumped over in the street. People standing by commented that they had never seen anything like it before.

One of the men said, "I knew that someday Mert's mouth would be the death of him.

One of the men standing by said, "Someone needs to get the sheriff!"

Another man commented, "It was more than a fair fight. Mert just kept badgering the stranger."

Mitch said, "I'll wait for the sheriff."

A few minutes later the sheriff arrived.

"I heard what happened. It sounds like it was self-defense. Come with me to my office. It's just down the street on the other side."

After discussing the matter with the sheriff and interviewing the eye witnesses, the sheriff decided to let Mitch go.

"Where are you staying in case I need to talk to you again?"

"Sheriff, I am staying at the Collins's place," Mitch replied.

"What are you doing out there with Maggie and her son? You know it doesn't look right to the townspeople—a young boy and a widow living with a stranger."

"Actually, it's none of your business. But for the record, I am working for Margaret Collins and am staying in the barn," Mitch walked back to the wagon and picked up the bag of grain and loaded it in the wagon.

"Here, mister, take this bag of grain to replace the one you lost." Mitch reached over and grabbed the bag of grain and placed it in the wagon.

"Just add this to my bill." He climbed up on the wagon and headed back to the ranch.

After supper Mitch explained to Maggie what had happened, and then he got up and walked to the barn to turn in. Maggie followed him out the door.

"Are you all right? I am sorry. I didn't think to ask earlier!"

"I am fine. Nothing happened to me. Good night, Maggie."

Over the next two weeks Mitch had cleaned up the place and repaired all of the fences. Now it looked like a real ranch again. The only thing left was to white wash the fences. One morning Mitch told Maggie he was going to town to pick up some white wash and asked if Trace wanted to ride along.

"Could I, Mom? Please I will be good!" Trace asked.

"Only if it is all right with Mitch."

"Why, sure, I would like to have some company and someone to talk to. Come on, son. Let's get going!"

Trace jumped on the wagon, and they headed out. After arriving in town Mitch pulled up in front of the Mercantile. He and trace went inside.

"Good morning, Ed," Mitch greeted.

"Who's you helper there," Ed asked.

"This is Trace, Maggie Collins's son."

"Nice to meet you, Trace. What can I do for the two of you today?" Ed asked.

"I need five buckets of white wash and some brushes to finish up the fences," Mitch replied. Ed yelled at a young man to help Mitch load the wagon.

"Is there anything else I can do for you?" Ed asked.

"You wouldn't by chance have a stick of candy around here, would you?"

"Of course I do, right over there," Ed pointed. "On the counter are two jars, son. Help yourself."

Trace turned to Mitch. "It's okay but don't take too many."

"Thank you, mister," Trace said.

"That's quite all right. Mitch, there is one thing I want to talk to you about in private. It will just take a few minute," Ed commented.

"Trace, could you wait in the wagon. I'll be out shortly."

"Yesterday, three men rode in that I have never seen before. They looked to me as if they were sizing up the town. It was hard to say. They spent a couple hours in the saloon then left in a big hurry, riding north. A short while later Billy Duggan, who works at the newspaper office, came by and said he recognized the three men. He said he had seen them in Pilgrim Creek a couple of years ago, before a terrible fire burned down the courthouse, killing the mayor and five members of the town council along with several other people inside. Billy said he saw those three men around the courthouse just before the fire, checking to make sure all the doors were locked. At first he didn't think much about it until the fire broke out. No one escaped. While the townspeople were busy putting out the fire, the bank was robbed, and two tellers were shot. That was the worst thing that had ever happened to the town. Oh, a posse was sent out, and they tracked the killers for a month but never picked up their trail again. The three men left town with three thousand dollars and were never seen again."

"Are you sure Billy is right about those men?" Mitch asked.

"If he said he recognized them, I believe him. He is not one for making up stories."

Without saying another word Mitch climbed upon the wagon and rode off at a brisk pace.

Ed yelled," Mitch! What's wrong? Do you know those men?"

Mitch and Trace kept on going without turning around.

"What's wrong?" Trace asked.

"Oh, nothing. Don't worry. Everything is going to be all right!"

The next day Mitch finished up some odd jobs around the ranch. The following morning Mitch told Maggie he would be gone for a few days but not to worry. He said he had some business to attend to and that could not wait.

"Can't you even tell me where you are going?" Maggie asked.

"I am sorry, but I can't. And thanks for everything," Mitch replied.

"It sounds like you are not coming back. It sounds more like a goodbye!" Maggie exclaimed.

"Don't go, Mitch," Trace asked.

"I am sorry, son, but I have to go. I don't have a choice."

Mitch got up from the table and walked out to the barn and grabbed his bedroll and opened his saddlebags. He pulled out a gun belt with a Colt revolver neatly tucked inside. He strapped it on then went outside and saddled his horse.

Maggie and Trace stood on the front porch of the little house and watched Mitch as he rode off. Mitch knew who these men were, and if he didn't do something right away, there could be a lot of killing. Mitch was on the outskirts of town when he heard a shot. He galloped closer to see what was happening. Down the street on the right side were three horses tied in front of the bank. Three men backed out of the bank, holding saddlebags; and then another shot rang out, this time killing a little girl standing by her mother inside the bank. The mother screamed and lunged toward for one of the killers. He turned and shot the woman in the head before she could get any closer.

One of the outlaws yelled, "Let's get the hell out of here before we have the whole town down on us!"

The sheriff ran up the street toward the bank with his gun drawn; before he could get off a shot, one of the outlaws turned and shot him in the leg, dropping him to the street. By now Mitch was in front of the bank, and the three killers were on their way out of town."

Mitch yelled out, "Stay out of the way! I will deal with the killers!" He kicked his horse in the flank, causing him to break into a run. After several hours in the saddle nightfall set in. He decided to wait until morning to follow the three men. At dawn the next day Mitch set out riding toward a small stand of Aspen where he could make out a small cabin directly behind them. He stopped and tied up his horse and circled behind the cabin.

There he saw the three horses tied up. These must be the killers! Mitch waited until dark before doing anything. He noticed one of the men heading toward the outhouse with a lantern in his hand. The man set the lantern down and closed the door behind him.

Mitch quietly approached the outhouse then jammed the door closed with a pine bow. He then picked up the lantern and shook out the kerosene around the outhouse then lit it with a match. Suddenly the fire ignited; within minutes, you could hear the man inside screaming and beating on the door, trying to get out. The two men inside the cabin came running out. One of them ripped open the door, but it was too late. The man inside was charred beyond recognition.

"Who in the hell did this? I am going to make him suffer when I get my hands on him!" one of the killers shouted. They went in opposite directions around the cabin, looking for any sign of someone that was there but found nothing.

"We will burn the damned town to the ground if we have to just like we did in Pilgrim Creek if we don't find out who did this." The two men decided to ride into town that night and find out who killed their friend.

"Joe, why don't you go into town, and I will catch up with you later. I want to bury what's left of Mert."

"Okay, I will meet you at the saloon."

It was dusk, and the road to town was darkened by rain clouds. First the wind began, followed by the rain. The rider decided to stop and wait for the storm to blow over. Behind him he heard the wind and something else. It was a lasso dropping over his head; suddenly his horse reared, throwing him to the ground.

The man on the ground yelled out, "Who are you?"

Without a word Mitch tied the man up; he walked over to his horse and pulled out a pair of heavy leather gloves and wire cutters from his saddlebag.

"What are you going to do?" the killer asked.

Mitch walked over to a barbed wire fence along the trail and cut off two long pieces of wire. Then he came back and wrapped the man up as tightly as he could while he was standing up, at the same time listening to his screams while the barbs cut into the man's skin. One end of the rope was tied to the man's hands extended out in front of him, and the other was tied to the saddle horn. He took his knife out and cut off the reins then smacked the horse on the rump, sending him on his way. The horse bolted, sending the man to the ground and dragging him at full speed toward town.

After the horse reached town several bystanders ran out in front of the horse to stop it. Because there were no reins a man grabbed the bridle, and another man grabbed the horse's head, slowly bringing him to a stop. The man dragged behind had a broken neck, and his body was cut to pieces.

"Look, this is one of the killers!" one of the men said.

Another person asked, "Who do you think did this?"

"I don't know but what a helluva a way to die," a man replied as he cut the rope from the saddle horn.

The sheriff hobbled over and said, "Get him off the street and cut off the barbed wire."

By now the other killer was on his way to town to meet his partner. He pulled up in front of the saloon, but there was no sign of his partner's horse. He swung open the saloon doors and looked around for his partner. There was no sign of him.

He then shouted, "I will kill everyone here unless someone tells me what happened to my friend!"

A voice in the wind said, "Outside, I will tell you where he is."

The killer turned away then walked outside but could see nothing. Then slowly the outline of a man stepped out of the shadows.

"I know what happened to both of your partners."

"Who the hell are you?"

"You don't remember me, but I was in the fire you and your partners set at Pilgrim Creek."

"That couldn't be. Everyone died in that fire," the killer uttered.

"Mister, that will be the last fire you ever set because I am going to kill you," Mitch replied.

The killer's eyes were as wide open as they could be, and sweat was running down his face. He knew he was standing in front of a dead man.

"I am going to let you draw first anytime you are ready."

The man was nervous but finally decided to reach for his gun; Mitch drew and shot him first in the right knee then fired again hitting him in the left knee. The man doubled over, screaming in pain. Mitch bent over and said, "This will give you some idea how it feels when you burn up in a fire."

The man looked up with fear in his eyes. Without further conversation Mitch shot the man between the eyes. The killer fell over backward onto the ground. Mitch walked over to the hitching post, untied his horse, and rode out of town.

The news of what happened spread throughout the town. There were many things that no one could figure out. Who was Mitch, and where did he come from?

The following day Maggie and Trace came to town to pick up a few things at the mercantile. As they were stepping down from the buckboard, Billy from the newspaper office came running toward them with something in his hand. "I just received this telegram, Mrs. Collins. I thought you might be interested in what it says. This is a list of everyone who died in the Pilgrim Creek fire. I want you to read the names out loud."

Maggie took the telegram from Billy and began reading the names. The last name on the list was Mitch Ranker.

WINTER OF DESPERATION

Saukannah was digging out wood from the fallen timber buried under two or more feet of snow. The tribe had exhausted its supply of wood for the winter, and it was only November. The winter had taken its toll with early snows and bitter cold temperatures. Not only was the supply of fire would be almost gone but also were the winter rations. No one had been able to hunt for fresh meat in over six weeks. The children's rations had been cut to two light meals a day along with the elderly. Five members of the tribe had died because of extreme cold and lack of food. It was as difficult to reach the livestock through the knee-deep snow and drifts. If Saukannah and others could not get out and hunt for fresh meat, many others would die before winter's end.

The temperatures were below 30 degrees, and it hovered at that mark for over three weeks. This was the worst winter in the past twenty years. After two hours of digging broken timber and branches out of the snow, Saukannah returned to the village and dropped wood in front of as many tepees as he could before going back for more. Saukannah worked late into the night gathering firewood for his village. He had his close friend, Adnokaway, help by holding a makeshift torch, lighting the way for Saukannah to see. After wood was provided for everyone in the village, Saukannah and Adnokaway fell quickly to sleep.

The next morning Saukannah and Adnokaway packed their hunting gear and started out on foot to hunt game for the village. They were armed with bows, arrows, and hatchets. That afternoon they came upon a small herd of deer, pawing to break the surface of the frozen snow and foraging for food under the deep hard pack.

Saukannah motioned for Adnokaway to circle around from behind while he tried to work his way closer for a better shot. Once Saukannah was in position he motioned for Adnokaway to prepare to shoot at the same time. There would only be one opportunity, and if neither made a kill, they would leave empty-handed.

Saukannah pulled an arrow form his quiver and placed on his bowstring. Adnokaway was now in position too. Saukannah sighted in on a large doe and released his arrow. It struck the doe in the neck, and she dropped to the ground. Unfortunately, Adnokaway's shot was high, missing its target and scaring the others off into the timber where they disappeared.

The two braves dressed out the doe then quartered it, enabling each of them to carry out a portion back to the village. Once they arrived back at the village, there was rejoicing and a prayer of thanks and gratitude for providing the meat. Saukannah and Adnokaway made one more trip each to bring back the two remaining quarters.

Over the next several days three more members of the tribe died—two young children and one of the elders. It became difficult for the tribe to keep up with the burials.

The burial site was about a mile away from the main village. Makeshift burials were used by digging out snow caves and placing each body inside and marking them until the ground thawed enough to erect the individual burial sites above ground.

It was the middle of December, and the weather still held its grip of death on the village.

The only thing that could be done was to hunt for more food and try to keep everyone warm until the weather let up. As time slowly progressed, some of the older members gave up hope and began chanting the death chant, just waiting to pass on.

Saukannah had to do something. He and Adnokaway had to find a way to help their people. Both of the braves had spent the past several days making sure every lodge had firewood to keep warm with. The main problem was still lack of food. Unless something was done right away, the tribe would all perish. Not only did their people need food, but they also need more robes for warmth. The babies' tiny faces were looking pallid and ghost-like due to lack of nourishment. The women could no longer provide milk because of their lack of nourishment. Saukannah decided that he and Adnokaway must do something before it was too late.

"Come with me, my brother. We will leave tomorrow in search of buffalo," Saukannah said to Adnokaway.

The next day the two braves left along with two packhorses in search of buffalo. The herd had not been seen since late summer. Since winter set in early the herd moved further south in search of food.

Adnokaway said, "We must be careful not to leave our people unprotected while we are away."

"You are right, but we have no choice. If we don't make it back with food and robes, our people will die anyway," Saukannah replied.

The snow was too deep for riding their ponies. They would lead them and the packhorses through the snow until they reached the lower elevation, slowly leaving the snow behind. One week had passed; they could see a valley far below, leading to a plateau and possibly taking them to the buffalo. Suddenly they heard shouting and saw a small herd of buffalo running directly toward them.

"What is happening? Why are the buffalo running towards us?" Saukannah shouted.

No sooner had Saukannah yelled than they saw another band of Indians driving the herd. They were making their kill and pushing the remainder of the herd further south.

"We must stay out of sight until they are gone!" Saukannah warned.

Some of the braves came close to be identified; they were Mandans. Saukannah and Adnokaway waited patiently until the squaws had field dressed, skinned, and tied the hides on the pack animals before leaving. It was safe to leave now and follow the herd further south, hoping not to run into the tribe. Saukannah and Adnokaway followed the herd south for about an hour before catching up with them. They left the horses behind a slope on the prairie and walked cautiously toward the herd, trying to get in bow range. To the left they saw a large bull with three arrows protruding from his side and back. The bull was staggering around before falling over on his side. Apparently he had been wounded by the Mandans and had just separated himself from the herd to die.

"Over here!" Saukannah pointed.

Adnokaway turned and saw the bull lying on his side. Both of the braves slowly approached the bull when suddenly they became surrounded by a band of Mandan braves.

The two braves attempted to retreat from the bull, but it was too late.

Saukannah approached the leader and said, "We are here because our people are weak and dying because of lack of food. We have come a long ways to find the buffalo and to feed our people. Our people were starving to death, and they desperately needed meat and robes to get through the winter."

After much discussion he was told that the Mandans were in search of food as well and that they had traveled much further west and north to find buffalo. The Mandans agreed to let Saukannah have the injured bull, but only if he and Adnokaway agreed to leave as soon as they were finished. Without further delay Adnokaway finished off the dying bull with one last arrow. Saukannah walked back to the ponies and brought them back to where the buffalo lay.

"I am going to bring back some branches to build a travois," Saukannah said.

Later Saukannah returned with several saplings to make the travois with. After the travois was made, two saplings were tied to one of the packhorse with rawhide. They tied on the buffalo quarters and hide, loading as much as the packhorse could carry before starting the long journey back. Three days of slow and hard riding put them back into the snowy area of the mountains where the ride became slower and more difficult. As they rode higher the snow became deeper.

The packhorse was near exhaustion; to give him rest, they moved the travois to the other packhorse before continuing on. After reaching a meadow on the south side of the mountain, Saukannah and Adnokaway mounted their horses and continued on toward the village. Suddenly Adnokaway's horse stepped into an ice-covered hole, throwing him off the horse. His horse rolled over on top of him crushing his hip. Adnokaway screamed; he was writhing in pain and could not move from underneath his horse. Saukannah jumped off his pony and went to Adnokaway.

Adnokaway looked up and said, "I am in a bad way. You better leave me and move on. There's nothing you can do for me."

"I am not going to leave you here to die. I will pull your pony off of you." Saukannah took a rope and threaded it though the double halter on Adnokaway's horse and the other two ends tied to the two pack horses. Saukannah tugged on the two horses slowly pulling Adnokaway's pony off of him. Adnokaway was free of his pony, but he could barely move his legs. Saukannah made a splint for Adnokaway's left side and a makeshift crutch to support him.

Saukannah helped Adnokaway to his feet, but Adnokaway could hardly move his feet one in front of the other. He was too badly injured; Adnokaway would have to be carried. The only choice was to leave the buffalo behind and place Adnokaway on the travois, taking him back to the village then returning for the buffalo.

Adnokaway spoke up, "You must leave me here. Meat for our people are more important than trying to save me!"

"I will not leave you here to die. Everything will work out," Saukannah replied.

Saukannah removed the buffalo from the travois and buried it under the snow at the base of a pine tree he blazed so that he could find it when he returned.

Saukannah dragged Adnokaway over to the travois and tied him on top.

Three days later it began to snow so much that Saukannah decided to stop and seek shelter in the forest. He covered Adnokaway with the only buffalo robe they had, then laid him under a large tree out of the wind and snow. Saukannah took the remaining blankets and wrapped himself up. It snowed all night long, and the wind was so fierce Saukannah could not see the horses or pony through the blizzard-like conditions. His main concern was to keep Adnokaway alive. Saukannah eventually fell asleep out of fatigue.

Several hours later he woke up and checked on Adnokaway. He shook Adnokaway, but he lay motionless; he froze to death during the night. Saukannah's heart sank; he had lost his best friend. After collecting his thoughts he buried Adnokaway in the snow at the base of the same tree he had placed him under the night before. He decided to leave Adnokaway and go back for the buffalo before continuing on to the village.

Two days later he picked up the buffalo, loading it back on the travois, and left for the village. The weather became worse; Saukannah knew he would have to seek shelter and wait for it to pass, or he would also die.

The braves had been gone for two weeks. Saukannah hoped that his people had not all perished waiting for his return. The storm started to let up, so he decided to continue on. His pony could travel no more and fell over dead from the extreme cold and from exhaustion. He was left with one pack animal and Adnokaway's pony. He had no idea how close he was to the village as the trail was covered over with drifted snow.

Later that week the snow stopped, and the sun appeared for the first time in days. The snow began to melt, making the journey a little easier. Saukannah had been walking for days looking at nothing but snow, which had taken its toll on his vision. He was experiencing snow blindness. He had to stop and rest his eyes and body before continuing on. He knew if he didn't, he may become permanently blind.

Two days later he was able to continue on. The only packhorse left could pull the travois no further, stopping in his tracks. Saukannah untied the travois from the horse and tied it on to the pony. This would be a great burden on a small pony, but there was nothing else that could be done. The days and nights became one.

Saukannah was obsessed in his effort to reach the village. He had to survive long enough to save his people. The weather had warmed considerably, making his efforts easier. There was one more mountain to cross before reaching the village. Saukannah's mind and soul was rejuvenated, knowing that the worst of the journey was over. He looked forward with great anticipation to reach the village and to rejoin his family and many friends once again.

After two days of hard climbing, Saukannah arrived at the top of the mountain where he could see the outline of the village far below. His heart beat with excitement, knowing he was nearly home. Saukannah led the pony and travois down the mountain, into a mountain meadow, and toward the village.

As he approached the village there was a strange feeling; there was no sign of life. He could not hear the sound of children playing nor could he see anything moving. Saukannah rode closer; suddenly he noticed bodies lying on each side of the trail. He stopped and jumped down from his pony to get a closer look. The first body he saw was an old friend; she had an arrow in her back and had been dead for some time. He bent over to examine the markings on the arrow; it was Blackfeet.

They must have attacked the village—driving many of his people out to run for their lives, trying to avoid being killed.

The scene became more gruesome as he rode into the village. The stench of death was everywhere. He was too late. The village had been ravaged by the Blackfeet, who must have swept down into the village taking everyone by surprise. The camp was strewn with dead bodies. The meat and everything else of value had been taken away.

Saukannah walked through the camp in disbelief, taking in the carnage. His hopes and dreams were gone. Not only had his best friend died, but his people had also been annihilated. He sat down between the decimation and cried for justice. The only justice there could be would be from him, and what could one man do against a tribe of Blackfeet? Saukannah made camp, and after several days he decided to leave.

He had prepared to leave when he saw a young woman step out of the wooded area west of the camp. It was Little Doe. His heart beat hope for the first time since he entered the village. He was not alone.

WINTER'S BLOOD

The snow was waist deep outside the cabin. It was difficult to reach the livestock to feed them. The hay was buried under the drifts, and the horses could not traverse the deep snow. The flat-roofed barn was covered with eighth-foot drifts. Inside the tiny cabin, supplies were running out. Someone had to walk to the outpost five miles away for provisions and then return.

Mar'chant and Penelope occupied the same cabin since Penelope was freed from a Crow warrior named Matchitehew, translated to mean "he has an evil heart," from a village high in the mountains a year before.

Penelope Rose was a young white girl originally taken by the Hidatsa following a raid on a small settlement, killing her father, mother, and younger brother. Later Penelope was traded to the Crow for ten horses. The women of the tribe scourged Penelope regularly because of her fair skin; she was not one of them. Mar'chant was a French trader and stole Penelope away from Matchitehew. Penelope had been held captive for seven years. Mar'chant and Penelope knew when the weather broke Matchitehew and the others would come looking for them. If they waited longer to leave for provisions, they would both starve to death. Mar'chant was better able to ward off an attack than Penelope. However, Penelope may not be strong enough to make the ten-mile trip to and from the trading post. Neither could wait for a break in the weather because the Crow would attack at once.

"I must go. You are the strong one. You can defend yourself better against the Crow than I can," Penelope said. Penelope strapped on makeshift snow shoes made from bent and dried willows sewn with strips of elk hide. She would not be able to carry much in the Crow saddlebags. The wind stopped howling; it was time for Penelope to leave.

Mar'chant gave her a hug and said, "May you find your way back to me."

"If I do not return in one week, you will know I am dead," Penelope said.

Penelope left the tiny cabin wrapped in a Hudson's bay blanket. The buffalo robe was too heavy for her to wear.

By the end of the first day Penelope had only walked two miles. She would have to prepare for the night. There was a small outcropping of rocks covered by a thicket of pines. The snow had blown over the rock face, creating a large snowdrift. Penelope pulled out her knife and began cutting through the drift, hollowing out a place to spend the night to protect her from the wind and snow. Once inside she was able to start a small fire by melting the snow and by drying out twigs which were lying beneath the snow cover. The next morning Penelope continued the arduous journey to the outpost.

The fourth day Penelope wandered into the small outpost and collapsed on the street, sick with fatigue and hunger. One of the women noticed Penelope lying motionless face down on the snow-covered street. The woman summoned her husband to help her move Penelope out of the street.

"Look, Ben, she is a beautiful young white woman dressed as an Indian."

"You are right, Bessie. Help me pick her up. We need to get her inside. She is shaking and crying. Let's put her in front of the fireplace in Lou's mercantile."

The two carried Penelope inside and laid her on blankets next to the large open fire, then covered her with a buffalo robe.

"The poor dear is half-frozen. She looks like she has been walking for days," Bessie said.

Several hours passed before Penelope could tell everyone who she was and why she had walked for days through blizzard conditions to find food and other supplies.

Penelope kept saying, "I need to get back before Mar'chant is killed by the Crow."

"Don't try to talk now. You need to regain your strength. We will move you to our cabin when you are well enough," Ben said.

"I can't wait that long. It is a matter of life and death," Penelope said.

Two days later Penelope was moved to Ben and Bessie's cabin where Bessie cared for her. Penelope was finally well enough to explain what had happened and why she needed to get back to Mar'chant as soon as possible.

"It would be certain death if you tried to walk the five miles back to the cabin in this weather. At least wait for the weather to break, and I will go with you," Ben said. The snow had stopped, and the sun was beginning to appear through the clouds.

Penelope said, "I can't wait any longer to leave. It might already be too late."

"If you insist on leaving now, I will go with you," Ben commented.

The days were still bitter cold, with snowdrifts standing between them and the tiny cabin. Toward nightfall at the end of the second day, they could make out the silhouette of the tiny cabin. There was one thing Penelope noticed; there was no fire or light coming from the cabin.

"We better be careful. We could be walking into a trap," Penelope said.

Ben took the lead and had his trigger cocked, ready to shoot. The two walked slowly up to the front of the cabin. The door was open, and snow had drifted inside. Penelope lit one of the kerosene lanterns hanging on the wall inside the doorway. She screamed at the horrific sight of dried blood everywhere. There were hand prints of blood on the doorframes and the tabletop.

Looking down, Ben kicked back the snow and saw dried bloodstains on the floor. It looked like someone had been dragged out the door. It was too dark to follow the bloody trail.

Penelope shouted, "We can't stay here! We will be killed too!"

"Penelope, there is nothing we can do. We will look for Mar'chant tomorrow. Whoever did this is long gone. We should be safe here for the night," Ben assured Penelope.

Early the next morning Ben and Penelope followed the path of blood in the snow. It had been so cold that the blood had clotted, leaving an easy trail. Suddenly the trail of blood stopped.

Ben said, "I will go ahead and see if there is any sign of Mar'chant. I want you to stay here. I will be back in a few minutes."

Ben walked ahead as the horror of what happened began to unfold before his eyes. On one side of the trail was Mar'chant's head, severed from his body—which had been hacked up, mangled, and then dumped on the other side of a bank of snow. There were tomahawk wounds and slashes covering his entire body.

Ben thought to himself, *What a gruesome way to die.* He could not let Penelope see Mar'chant's remains and how he died. Ben returned to Penelope and told her there was no sign of Mar'chant; they must have taken him away.

"In the spring we will return and look further for Mar'chant. There is nothing we can do now," Ben said.

Penelope was sickened by the thought that she was to blame for Mar'chant's death and that Matchitehew would come looking for her again someday. Penelope was free, but she was haunted by what might have happened to Mar'chant. She knew she would never be at peace until she found the answer; she had a deep love for Mar'chant and couldn't get him out of her mind.

After returning to the outpost, Penelope went to work at a clothing and millinery store for a woman named Isabelle Mestas. Penelope was treated well and was even considered part of the family. Time passed, and Penelope was still thinking about Mar'chant.

One day Penelope approached Mrs. Mestas. "I need to go away for a while, but I would like to have my job back when I return. Please don't tell anyone," Penelope asked.

"Where will you go, and what are you planning to do?" Mrs. Mestas asked.

"I am sorry, but I can't tell you. It has to do with my past and a man that was an important part of my life, that's all I can tell you."

"Please don't leave, Penelope, let me help you. You will need money and a good horse and supplies. I will provide these things for you but only if you promise to return after you have found your answers," Mrs. Mestas said.

Penelope reluctantly accepted the offer and prepared to leave the outpost. It would take Penelope several days to locate the Crow encampment, depending on where it had been moved to. The trail leading up the mountain was narrow and treacherous with shale cliffs hanging on one side. In places, the trail was so narrow that you could only walk your horse behind you.

The second day Penelope had reached the narrow part of the trail covered with shale as well. Penelope climbed down from her horse and led him slowly up the winding mountainside. Her horse started to slide backward on loose shale. Penelope tried to calm him down. He jerked the reins from her hands and lost his balance. He screamed as he plunged down the steep cliff to the river below.

Everything was gone—her blankets, food, and water, along with other clothing. Penelope was about halfway from the top; it was too late to turn back, so she decided to continue on.

Later that afternoon she came across a small stream crossing the trail in front of her. She stopped to drink but had nothing to carry water in. Penelope had lived among the Crow long enough to adjust to whatever situation she was in. She stopped for the night but needed something to eat.

Off the trail was a small plateau with bushes of berries on them. They were huckleberries, and they would serve as her meal. After eating what she wanted she picked more and laid them out on a flat area to dry. She would take them along for food. She made a small carrier out of wild grass and leaves to carry the berries in. Penelope climbed further and further up the mountainside. She finally reached the summit where she could see for miles.

There was no sign of the crow encampment. Penelope started across the mountain meadow, walking toward the forest. Before entering the forest she decided to look for any sign of the Crow. Looking at the trees in the middle of the forest, she noticed an area where several horses and people had entered, scrubbing the bark off. This must be Crow moving to a different location. The following morning Penelope continued on through the dense forest until she could make out a trail of smoke on the horizon.

"This must be the Crow encampment," Penelope thought. If it was, how could she approach the Crow? She could only walk in and hope she wasn't killed before meeting with Matchitehew. Penelope slowly approached the encampment. Before she came any closer several braves came running toward her. They grabbed her by the arms and dragged her in front of a teepee, throwing her on the ground.

"I want to speak with Matchitehew!" Penelope kept repeating.

Matchitehew stepped out of the teepee. "You came back! Why are you here? You know I will kill you if you try to escape again!" Matchitehew said.

"I came back to find out what you did to Mar'chant, that'all," Penelope said, raising his voice.

"You are a fool. I killed Mar'chant by cutting off his head and leaving it in the snow. He betrayed my trust by taking you from me."

Penelope now realized that Ben had found Mar'chant's body but did not want her to see it. Matchitehew motioned for Penelope to come closer. With strong reservation Penelope walked toward him.

As she came close enough Matchitehew reached out and grabbed Penelope by the hair. While staring in her eyes, he said, "You are mine, and no one will ever take you from me again."

A cage was built, and Penelope was placed inside like a wild animal. She was given water and scraps to eat along with the camp dogs.

Penelope kept screaming, "Please let me out of here! I won't run away!"

It had been three days since Penelope had been placed in the cage.

Matchitehew walked up to the cage and unlocked the latch and said, "If you try to run off I will put you back in the cage for the rest of your life."

Penelope knew that she had made a terrible mistake and that she would never be able to leave. Instead of the cage, a collar with a rope tied to it was placed around Penelope's neck, and the end of the rope was tied to a stake driven deep in the ground. This wasn't much better than the cage. Each time the Crow women passed by they would whip or torment her.

Two weeks passed. One morning Matchitehew came to Penelope and removed the collar from around her neck and said, "Today you will be my wife."

Penelope said, "I will never be your wife after the way you have treated me."

Matchitehew slapped Penelope in the face, knocking her to the ground. Penelope slowly picked herself up then suddenly pulled Matchitehew's knife from his scabbard.

She backed off and said, "You will never hurt me again. If you come any closer I will kill myself!" Matchitehew laughed and started toward Penelope, but before he reached her, she took the knife with both hands and plunged the blade into her heart.

Penelope fell to the ground dead.

TOO SAD TO CRY

Terrel stood on the boardwalk in front of the stage stop, waiting for the eight thirty from Butte.

His heart beat with excitement. He was waiting for his mail order bride, whom he had never met, arriving from Dead Wood. Terrel was a tall lean-looking man with a heavy dark beard and hair. He wore a worn out black Stetson, and boots. Terrel was average in looks with a kind disposition.

This was the last leg of Cora's journey to Kalispell. Terrel had corresponded with Cora Wandel for over a year. He found her information in a mail order bride publication. This was the day Cora was to arrive and take Terrel as her husband. Cora had been raised by an aunt following the death of her father and mother, leaving her alone at age twelve. Cora became very independent at a young age, but she was tired of the corruptness and way of life in Dead Wood and was looking for a fresh start in Kalispell.

The stage was late, and the weather began to change with falling rain and winds whipping up out of the south. Terrel was becoming concerned! Had something happened, or was the stage just running behind? Suddenly Terrel heard the sound of horses and wheels rolling over the hard packed main street into Kalispell.

"Whoa, you lazy critters! When I want you to go you stop, and when I want you to stop you go!" the stage driver yelled. The stage pulled up in front of the stage depot where Terrel and several other people were standing, waiting for the passengers to get off.

"Why so late?" Terrel asked.

"You know that area around Devil's Gulch? It was so slick we had to slow down and make sure the stage stayed on the road," the driver said.

"I'm glad you made it with everyone safe," Terrel said A plain-looking woman with hair neatly tucked under her western hat, dressed in jeans and cowboy boots, stepped off the stage. She was the only woman resembling Cora's description.

Terrel stepped forward, removing his hat and said, "You must be Cora?"

"Yes, I am. And you must be Terrel," the woman replied.

"I'm Terrel Hawkins. I am proud to meet you," he said as he reached out to shake Cora's hand.

Cora stepped up and gave Terrel a big hug and said, "Don't you think after all this time you can do better than shake my hand?"

"I suppose you are right, but it seems like we really don't know each other yet. I guess I am a little shy, that's all."

"If I am to be your bride we need to start acting like we at least like each other, don't you think?" Cora said.

"Of course we do. I am sorry. I have never done anything like this before!"

Cora's baggage was now on the ground, waiting to be picked up. "Wait right here. I will bring the wagon around. I'll grab your baggage then we will head to the ranch."

Terrel walked around the corner where the wagon was hitched and brought it around where Cora was standing by her bags.

Terrel loaded Cora's baggage, then they rode off toward Terrell's small ranch about two miles west of town.

"You know, Cora, the ranch isn't that much, but it's all mine. I inherited it from my grandfather when he passed on a while back," Terrel said.

"I am sure it is a fine ranch. This part of the country is so beautiful," Cora said.

The timber-clad road lined its way to the open space leading to the ranch. The main house sits on a hill overlooking a winding river to the south, with sprawling mountains to the north that could be seen twenty miles away.

"This is the most beautiful country I have ever seen, and the view from the ridge is spectacular!" remarked Cora.

"I certainly hope you like living out here. I have tried to keep everything in order. I have been cooking for myself for years. I'm not use to anything fancy, just meat and potatoes."

"Well, I believe I may even be able to improve upon your diet," Cora said as she laughed.

"Cora, I want you to take the bedroom, and I will sleep out on the floor in front of the fireplace until we become better acquainted, if that's all right with you," Terrel said.

After Terrel had brought Cora's baggage inside he noticed Cora taking off her hat and shaking her hair out, letting it fall down around her shoulders. Terrel knew he had made the right choice. Cora was everything and more that he had hoped for in a wife.

The next morning Cora said, "When do you think we should get married?"

"I hadn't thought much about it. After all this is so soon. We just met for the first time yesterday."

"I think we should get married today. Otherwise, what are people in town going to say about us living together like this?" Cora suggested.

"I suppose you're right."

That afternoon Cora and Terrel went to town to find the preacher. They pulled up in front of the church and found the preacher working on a new addition.

"What can I do for the two of you?" the preacher asked as Cora and Terrel walked inside the church.

"Preacher, my name is Terrel Hawkins, and this is my wife-to-be, Cora Wandel. We would like you to marry us today."

"Wait a minute, young man. Why in such a hurry? You have the rest of your lives to be married! By the way, I am Father Fondulay, and I will be happy to assist the two of you. But first, tell me about yourselves."

After explaining how they met Father Fondulay agreed to marry them. They were married in front of the sheriff, Pete Drugger, and his wife, Martha, who were good friends of Terrel. Over the next year Cora and Terrel became inseparable; wherever you saw one, the other was nearby. One day Cora told Terrel they were expecting their first child.

Terrel was so excited he told Cora, "Get your finest clothes on. We are going to town to celebrate!"

Into town they went, where they ended up at the Bear Head Saloon.

"Drinks are on me, everyone!" Terrel yelled. "We are going to have a baby!"

Everyone came up to Cora and Terrel and congratulated them.

This was the happiest day of their lives. Following the celebration, Cora and Terrel rode back to the ranch.

"You know, Cora, when I first met you, I wasn't sure if you were the right one. But now I know you are, and I couldn't love you more," Terrel said.

"I feel the same way. I never expected to find this kind of happiness in my life."

Following the birth of Lilly, their firstborn, Cora and Terrel were the proudest parents in all of Montana. Two years later came a second child. This time it was a boy, who they named Cole. A year later Cora gave birth to another girl whom they named Etta.

As time went by, Lilly had become the focal point in Terrell's life. She followed her father around, observing everything he did. They appeared to be closer than the other children. It was not that Lilly was loved any more than the others; it was just that she was always with Terrel. She became old enough to learn how to milk the cows which was a real challenge for such a young girl. To show Lilly his trust he gave her one of the Holsteins to milk and care for. She was to milk her twice a day and make sure she had plenty of hay and cared for. Lilly couldn't be happier. She looked forward each day to care for the cow that she named Dollie.

One evening after supper Lilly said, "I forgot to milk Dollie. I guess I was out riding too long."

"It is too late to go out to the barn. I will milk her this time but don't forget again," Terrel told her.

"Please, Daddy, let me milk her. I will be careful. I know what to do," Lilly begged.

"Why don't you let her this one time? It won't take her too long," Cora said.

"Okay, but be careful out there and don't set the bucket too close to Dollie's feet, or she could kick it over," Terrel told Lilly.

"Thanks, Ma and Pa. I will be back before you know it," Lilly replied.

Lilly walked out to the barn where Dollie was standing in one of the stalls, bawling because she needed to be milked. Lilly made sure Dollie was securely tied to one side of the stall before reaching for the milk pale.

The wind began to blow, banging the door of the barn. Lilly walked to the front of the barn and latched the door closed to keep it in place.

It was dark inside, especially with the door closed. Lilly had watched her dad light the kerosene lantern many times. She reached up and removed the lantern from its hook hanging from one of the beams. After lighting it she laid it down next to Dollie. Lilly sat down on the three-legged stool ready to start milking.

Suddenly, something startled Dollie, and she kicked the stool over along with Lilly. Lilly fell on the ground, knocking over the lantern into the nearby hay. The lantern ignited the hay then the barn as the kerosene poured out. The barn was now engulfed in flame. Dollie was bawling, and Lilly panicked. Lilly made her way to the front of the barn but could not get the barn door open after unlatching it. The wind was blowing directly toward the door, preventing her from pushing it open.

Inside the house Terrel caught a glimpse of flames coming from the barn. He jumped up and yelled, "Lilly is out there, and the barn is on fire!"

Cora told the two children to stay in the house. She and Terrel ran to the barn. It took both of them to force the door open against the wind. Lilly was lying inside the door on the ground, lifeless. Terrel reached down and picked her up.

Her eyes opened briefly and she said, "I am sorry, Daddy." Then her body went limp. She was gone.

Terrel and Cora pulled Lilly up into their arms, holding her and sobbing until neither could shed more tears.

Terrel and Cora blamed themselves for several years following Lilly's death. Terrel was never quite the same afterward; a part of him lay in the grave alongside Lilly. Terrel refused to go to town for a long time. He lived with the fear that something could happen to the other two children if he wasn't with them. Cora had to run most of the errands, taking the wagon to town for supplies and everything else. Terrel had withdrawn from the townspeople who tried to help. He was still too grief-stricken and unwilling to receive any help. Only time would heal the open wound in his heart. Time passed, and with all things, Terrel learned to live with the death of Lilly.

One day Cora came to Terrel and said, "I have thought about leaving the ranch for a while and going back to Deadwood to visit some of my old friends. It will give both of us time away from each other and help us heal. Maybe when I return it will give both of us a fresh start."

"I don't want you to go. You know much I will miss you. But if it is your wish then I suppose it would be selfish of me to say no. How long do you plan on being away?" Terrel asked.

"I am not sure. It may be a month, maybe two. I will let you know before I come back," Cora replied.

"The one concern I have is taking care of the children. I need to work the ranch and see after them as well."

"I thought about that too, and I asked Martha Drugger if she could come out a couple days a week and give you a hand with the children. Since she and Pete have no children of their own, she thought it would be a fine idea and was more than willing to help out."

Cora spent the next two days getting everything ready for her trip but also for the children. She made sure their clothes were clean and their bedding changed. The house was cleaned from top to bottom, and Cora had the children bring in the firewood and stack it up for winter. It was September, and Cora wanted to leave before winter set in.

Terrel was concerned; he had never been alone with the children without Cora. The next day all four left for town. Cora's stage was scheduled to leave at nine five. Terrel threw Cora's baggage up to the shotgun rider. He tied it down on the top and covered it with canvas.

It was time for Cora to leave. Terrel along with Cole and Etta gave Cora hugs and kisses. The children were both crying; they didn't want to see their mother leave.

Terrel stepped up. "We will all miss you terribly, but I hope you have a safe trip and return to us as soon as possible. We all love you very much," Terrel said as he held Cora in his arms and gave her one last kiss before leaving.

Cora was crying as well and said, "I love you all, and I will miss you and think of you every day until I return."

Terrel helped Cora on the stage then closed the door in front of him, then waved goodbye along with the children. Terrel and the children watched until the stage was out of sight. They got in the wagon and headed back to the ranch. It was a sad night; everyone was missing Cora, especially the children.

Every Wednesday and Friday, Martha would ride out to the ranch and spend each day cleaning and cooking for Terrel and the children.

This gave him more time to get everything ready for the long winter. Four weeks passed with no word from Cora.

Terrel thought that she should be in Deadwood by now. He would send a telegram but he didn't know anyone in Deadwood to whom he would he send. The following week Terrel watched as the sheriff, Pete Drugger, rode toward him.

"Hi, Sheriff. What brings you out this way? I was expecting Martha."

"I told Martha to stay home today. There is something I need to talk to you about."

"Well, come on in. Let's go in the house where it is more comfortable, Pete."

"Terrel, what I've got to say is not going to be pleasant anyway."

"What do you mean? Just spit it out."

Pete reached in his vest pocket and pulled out a telegram then handed it to Terrel.

"Here. You read this, and then you will know why I am here."

Terrel began to read the telegram when his knees buckled beneath him.

Cora was dead. She had been killed in a stage holdup outside of Deadwood. The telegram went on to say she was apparently killed when one of the outlaws asked everyone to hand over all of their valuables. Cora reached in her purse, and the outlaw standing by her shot her in the head, thinking she had a gun. Cole and Etta were playing outside by the corral. Terrel fell to the ground in disbelief with both hands over his head.

"How could this happen? She was a wonderful wife and mother! What am I going to do without her?" Terrel was too shocked to cry; he was distraught and overcome with emotions. Pete tried to console Terrel, but it did no good. Terrell's state of mind was somewhere else.

"Terrel, Martha asked me to invite you and the children over to our place for a while until you decide what you want to do."

Pete stood up, "You know our hearts go out to you and the children, and if we can do anything at all, we would like to help. Please think over our offer and just come up to the house when you are ready."

Terrel sat in the house with his head in his hands for several hours trying to sort through everything. Etta came inside and asked Terrel if he was all right.

"Honey, go get your brother and come back as fast as you can."

Moments later Etta returned with Cole. Terrel sat the children down and tried to explain to them that their mother was not coming back and that she was dead. The children didn't know what to think. They both broke down in tears, crying profusely. Their mother had always been there for them, and now she was gone forever.

The next morning Terrel gathered the children and packed some clothes then rode out to Pete and Martha's ranch.

"I need to go to Deadwood and bring Cora's body back to be buried here. Would you mind watching the children until I return?" Terrel asked Pete and Martha.

"Of course we will. You take as much time as you need, Terrel, and we will be here when you return," Martha replied.

Terrel left Kalispell and returned six weeks later with Cora's body lying in a lead-lined casket to help keep it preserved until it could be placed in the ground. Cora was buried alongside Lilly with both graves overlooking the river.

Though Terrel still had two beautiful children given to him by Cora, life could never be the same. Terrel started to spend more time in town, drinking at one of the two saloons. Pete and Martha watched as Terrel slowly changed, becoming less interested the children and the ranch and looking forward to each day in town getting drunk. Martha took it upon herself to ride out to the ranch each day and watch over the children, seeing that they were fed and had clean clothes to wear.

Pete told Martha, "I can't just sit here and watch Terrel destroy his life by climbing inside a whiskey bottle and staying there."

"What are you going to do?" Martha replied.

"I am going to sit him down and have a heart-to-heart talk. He needs to understand his responsibilities as a man and father. He still has much to be grateful for."

"Terrel, I want to talk to you in private," Pete said.

Terrel lifted his head off the table with a glass of whiskey in each hand. "This is private enough for me. Go ahead and say whatever's on your mind, Sheriff," Terrel replied in a slurred voice.

"I want you to start acting like a man instead of a drunk. Another thing, you need to think about your two beautiful children. They need their dad more than ever now."

"Just leave me alone! I can take care of everything just fine," Terrel replied before passing out on the table. Pete loaded Terrel in the wagon and took him back to the ranch and put him to bed.

Meanwhile the children were being cared for by Martha at the ranch. The next day Terrel rode over to Pete's ranch, apologized for his behavior, and thanked him and Martha for caring about him and the children and helping them out.

"I will be taking the children back to the ranch now," Terrel said.

"If you need anything at all don't hesitate to let us know, and Martha will be over in the next couple of days to check on you."

Back at ranch without prior conversation, Terrel told the children to pack their clothes and that he was taking them to visit an aunt they had never met in Oregon. Cole and Etta were excited. This would be a welcome change. Following two weeks of rough riding by stagecoach they arrived in Salem, Oregon.

"Is this where our aunt lives?" Cole asked.

"It sure is. We will be there shortly."

They were in a rented carriage, riding out to a large stone building with high fences all around. They drove through the wide open gates, down a long driveway leading to the front of the building. As they drew closer two men dressed in white greeted them. After the carriage stopped the men removed the baggage from the carriage.

Suddenly, fear ran through the minds of the children; they knew this was not their aunt's home but was a place where children are put when no one else wants them.

"Well, children here we are. This will be your new home. What do you think?"

Cole and Etta looked at each other and then their dad, and they started to cry.

"Everything will be just fine. Please go with the nice men," Terrel told them.

Etta ran back to Terrel and said, "Please don't leave me here, Daddy! I'm so scared!"

Without uttering a word, Terrel climbed back in to the carriage and left. Terrel arrived back in Kalispell without the children. Everyone asked about Cole and Etta. Terrel told them they were doing well, living with their aunt in Salem, Oregon.

Two years went by, and Terrel could barely lift his head up long enough to say hello to anyone, let alone talk about the children He had become a full-fledged drunk. The ranch fell into disrepair, and the crops dried up and blew away. The livestock eventually ran off or died of starvation with no one to care for them. Six months later Terrel died of liver problems. He had drunk himself to death.

Pete and Martha saw to it that he was laid to rest next to Cora and Lilly on the beautiful hill overlooking the river.

ALTERNATIVE ENDING TO: TOO SAD TO CRY

Though Terrel still had two beautiful children given him by Cora, life could never be the same. Terrel started to spend more times in town, drinking at one of two saloons. Pete and Martha watched as Terrel slowly changed, becoming less interested in the children and the ranch along with looking forward to each day in town getting drunk. Martha took it upon herself to ride out to the ranch each day and watch over the children, seeing that they were fed and had clean clothes to wear.

Pete told Martha, "I just can't sit here and watch Terrel destroy his life by climbing inside a whiskey bottle and staying there."

"What are you going to do?" Martha asked.

"I am going to sit him down and have a heart-to-heart talk. He needs to understand his responsibilities as a man and father. He still has much to be grateful for."

"I want to talk to you in private," Pete said.

Terrel lifted his shed off the table with a glass of whiskey in each hand. "This is private enough for me. Go ahead and say whatever's on your mind, Sheriff," Terrel replied in a slurred voice.

"I want you to start acting like a man instead of a drunk. Another thing, you need to think about your two beautiful children. They need their dad more than ever now."

"Just leave me alone! I can take care of everything just fine," Terrel replied before passing out on the table. Pete loaded Terrel in to the wagon and took him back to the ranch and put him in bed.

Meanwhile the children were being cared for by Martha at the ranch. The next day Terrel rode over to Pete's ranch, apologized for his behavior, and thanked him and Martha for caring about him and the children and helping them out.

"I will be taking the children back to the ranch now," Terrel said.

"If you need anything at all, don't hesitate to let us know, and Martha will be over in the next couple of days to check on you."

Without prior conversation, Terrel told the children to pack their clothes and that he was taking them to visit an aunt they had never met in Oregon. Cole and Etta were excited. This would be a welcome change. Following two weeks of rough riding by stagecoach they arrived in Salem, Oregon.

"Is this where our aunt lives?" Cole asked?

"It sure is. We will be there shortly."

They were in a rented carriage, riding out to a large stone building with high fences all around. They drove through the wide open gates, down a long driveway leading to the front of the building. As they drew closer two men dressed in white greeted them. After the carriage stopped the men removed the baggage from the carriage.

Suddenly, fear ran through the minds of the children; they knew this was not an aunt's home but was a place where children are put when no one wants them.

"Well, children, here we are. This will be your new home. What do you think?"

Cole and Etta looked at each other and then their dad, and they started to cry.

"Everything will be just fine. Please go with the nice men," Terrel told them.

Etta ran to Terrel and said, "Please don't leave me here, Daddy! I'm so scared!"

Without uttering a word Terrel climbed back into the carriage and left. Terrel arrived back in Kalispell without the children.

Many of the townspeople inquired about Cole and Etta. Terrel told everyone they were doing well, living with an aunt. Pete and Martha weren't convinced that everything was well with the children. Terrel had never spoken of taking the children to live with an aunt in Oregon before.

Over the next several months, no one saw much of Terrel as he stayed on his ranch trying to maintain everything and making sure his livestock were taken care of during the winter months. Occasionally he would come to town for supplies, but he never stayed long. Terrel would have a drink or two but never left town drunk as he had in the past.

"You know, Martha, it looks like Terrel is getting life together after all," Pete said.

"It looks like it, but I still don't know what happened with the children. That still seems odd to me."

"If the weather lets up, I think I will ride out tomorrow and pay Terrel a visit."

The next day Pete rode out to Terrell's ranch. Pete climbed down from his horse and walked up to the front door. Terrel saw him coming and greeted him on the porch.

"Come on in, Pete. It's too cold to stand outside. What brings you out in weather like this, anyway?" Terrel asked.

"Oh, I just thought I would come by and see how you were doing, that's all. We haven't seen much of you in town or at our place since you returned from Salem. Is something bothering you?"

"Now why do you ask? Everything is going as well as it can."

"There is something I've had on my mind for a long time that's been eating at me, and I wanted to talk to you about it, Terrel."

"What is it? You know we can talk about anything that's bothering you. We've known each other for a long time, Pete."

"You never spoke of an aunt in Oregon before you up and took the children to Salem and left them. Personally I think something else is going on, but it may be none of my business though."

"Well, Pete, you are right. And I won't lie to you. I didn't feel I could properly care for Cole and Etta and run the ranch after Cora died, so I made arrangement with an orphanage in Salem to let them live there until I got back on my feet. I know it sounds like a terrible thing I did. I just didn't know what else to do without involving you or anyone else in my problems."

"Terrel, that answers a lot of mine and Martha's concerns. However, I wished you had told us! You know we would have taken the children until you were able to handle them again."

"Pete, my plans are to bring the children back as soon as I can. I figure by next year I might be in a position to do that if everything goes along as planned."

"Let Martha and I know when you are ready, and we will go with you if you like."

"I would appreciate that, Pete. You and Martha are the best friends anyone could have."

"One more thing. Laurel Mercell's niece has come to Kalispell to stay the summer. Martha and I are having them over for dinner tomorrow and we wanted to invite you too."

"I would be honored to have dinner with you and meet Laurel's niece. What time shall I be there?"

"About eight o'clock, and Laurel's niece's name is Emily Sauder. She came all the way from Topeka. She looks about your age."

"I will see you tomorrow then."

The next day Terrel was excited and filled with anticipation in meeting Laurel's niece. This would be the first time he had gotten out and met anyone since Cora's death. That evening Terrel rode over to Pete and Martha's place for dinner. Terrel was introduced to Emily; it appeared they had a lot in common, though Emily had never been married and could not have children of her own. After dinner, Terrel asked Emily if she would like to take a walk around the ranch. Emily was very excited and readily agreed to go with Terrel. Over the summer Terrel spent much time with Emily in town and at the ranch. There was something special about her, a sweetness that he hadn't experienced since losing Cora.

For the first time in several years Terrel was falling in love again. Emily was smitten with Terrel and felt sorry for what he had gone through, losing Lilly and his wife Cora.

Terrel hadn't told Emily about Cole and Etta at the orphanage. It was near the end of summer, and Emily had decided to stay longer. She had strong feelings for Terrel, who was one of the few men in her life she had ever felt this way about. Emily made arrangements with her aunt to stay longer, then she told Terrel of her plans. Terrel was excited and decided to ask Emily to marry him, and Emily accepted.

"You know, Emily, I thought I would never love another woman again until you came into my life. I love you very much, and I hope we have a lasting marriage."

"I love you too. But there is one thing you need to know. I can never have children. How do you feel about that?"

"That is not a problem. There is something else you need to know. I have two children in an orphanage in Salem, Oregon, who I couldn't care for after my wife died. I have a boy named Cole and a daughter named Etta. I think of them every day, and I am sickened by the fact I was unable to care for them and took them to an orphanage."

"That is wonderful. Why don't we bring them back to Kalispell where we can raise them together?"

"Would you do that? That is taking on a lot, especially just getting married and all."

"Yes, I would. Let's go to Oregon as soon as we can. I am so excited, and I really want to do this. I promise I will be the best mother possible. I know I can't take Cora's place, but I can still be a good mother to them."

After telling Pete and Martha about their plans, Terrel and Emily left for Oregon. Following a long and hard ride by stagecoach they arrived in Salem. They rode toward the orphanage in a rented carriage.

"Well, what do you think of this place?" Terrel asked Emily.

"I think it is a cold place with beautiful grounds. I hope the inside is more desirable than the outside."

They parked the carriage and walked in the large front doors that led down a long hallway. They were greeted by a member of the staff.

"May I help you?" a woman asked.

"Yes, I am Terrel Hawkins, and this is my wife, Emily. We have come for my two children. You should have received my letter letting you know some time ago."

"May I have the names of your children?" the woman asked.

"Yes, my son's name is Cole, and my daughter's name is Etta. They have been here about three years."

"Please have a seat here in the waiting area, and I will be back in a few minutes."

An hour later the woman returned and told them there was only a daughter there and that the son had passed away over a year ago.

"How can this be? When I dropped them off they were both in good health, and why didn't someone let me know?"

"We had no way to contact you until we received your letter. When you left the children with the orphanage, you left no address or any way of contacting you," the woman told Terrel. "According to our records, Cole died of pneumonia, following congestion in both lungs. The doctor did everything he could, but nothing seemed to work. Your son is buried out back behind the carriage house, along with the others who have passed away. A marker is placed on each grave. If you like I can take you there, and you may look for the grave."

Terrel grabbed Emily's hand and followed the woman outside to the gravesite. After searching the grounds they finally came across Cole's gravesite. Terrel was in shock. He had lost another child because of his own doings rather than accepting his responsibilities. Emily tried her best to comfort him, but nothing seemed to help.

"If you wish, I will bring your daughter to the waiting area along with her belongings. Please give me a few minutes."

"I would appreciate that," replied Terrel. Later the woman along with Etta returned.

When Etta first set eyes on her father, she wasn't sure of what to think. It had been over three years since she had seen him; he never came once to visit.

"It is me, Etta. Please forgive me forever for having brought you here. This is Emily, my new wife and your new stepmother. We have come to take you home."

Following mixed emotions, Etta walked slowly toward her father. Terrel reached down and picked her up, giving her a hug and kisses.

"I have thought about you and your brother every day and have missed you both desperately. Can you find a way in your heart to forgive me?"

Etta was the last living memory of Cora and her loving contribution.

"Yes, I will try to forgive you. But it could take a long time," Etta replied.

The three left the orphanage and Salem then returned to Kalispell, where they lived out their lives.

Two years later, Terrel died of a liver disease, which was a result of his past drinking. Emily raised Etta and treated her as her own until she passed on.

SHADOWS OF DARKNESS

"I am so excited that I will finally be able to meet your brother Mitch after waiting for more than two years, "Jodi stated.

"It seems like much longer to me. I hope the wind calms down so that the welcome home banner doesn't blow down before Mitch arrives tomorrow. 1'Trent replied.

Mitch was to arrive in town the next day by stage around noon. Mitch had been in a hospital for several months before being released from a Confederate hospital after receiving The Purple Heart. Mitch lost his left arm from shrapnel wounds while saving five men in his column. The townspeople along with his brother Trent and his wife Jodi were anxiously waiting his return. The town had built picnic tables and lined each side of Main Street. This was a special celebration and the local people wanted to express their appreciation for the price Mitch paid and for his service. The wind had been blowing for several days but seemed to be slowing now.

The following morning the Ladies from everywhere brought their prepared meals of fried chicken and all the side dishes. A side of beef had been turning all night on a homemade spit made by Jess Higgins, who owned the hardware store. The morning was cool with mild light falling; however, day break left a calming breeze as the sun began to break through the over cast sky. Everyone had filled each side of the street waiting for the stage to arrive. The stage was running late.

Jodie said. I'm getting concerned Trent.

"Don't be concerned, it runs late most of the time, I'm sure it will be hear short ly." Every one's eyes were fixed on the dusty road leading into town. Suddenly the stage began to appear over the horizon kicking up dust as it rolled into town. The streets were lined with well-wishers shouting, "Welcome home Mitch"! The stage pulled up in front of the station and everyone waited impatiently for Mitch to climb out. This was a historical day in the small town of Hawk Springs. Mitch was the first survivor of the Civil War to come home. Two passengers climbed out followed by Mitch. There was a roar of cheering and laughter as Mitch looked around at everyone. The stage driver handed down Mitch's two leather worn bags filled with all his personal belongings.

Trent greeted him with a hug and said. 11Welcome home brother, I am so glad to see you. By the way, and this is my Wife Jodi".

"It is my pleasure mam, it looks like the two of you are very happy, Mitch," remarked. Jodi grabbed Mitch around the neck and gave him a big hug.

"You know Mitch you were all that Trent talked about while you were gone and please just call me Jodi. I look forward to having you in our lives," Jodi said. It had been over two years since Mitch had joined the Confederate forces. Mitch spent that afternoon eating and talking to everyone about his tour in the war and how he lost his arm . The festivities went on for two day before everyone returned to their normal daily activities.

"Well brother, what are your plans now that your back, Trent asked?

"I'm not sure, are you still living at the old homestead or are you living in town?" Mitch asked.

"I moved to town after ma and pa passed away. I couldn't work the old place alone. It was too much for one person and I couldn't afford to hire anyone. I moved back to town and went to work at the feed and supply store. In fact, that's where I met Jodi. John Slater the owner gave us a place to live above the store until we could get on our feet," Trent replied.

"I'm going to ride out to the old home stead and see if I can work it for a while. I don't have any other plans right now; I saved up a few dollars to tide me over "Mitch said.

Trent replied, "I think you are crazy, especially without two hands. though I can help you on Sundays, that's the only day I have off."

"Don't worry; I can do more than most men with two hands. I've had no choice but to learn how to get by," Mitch replied. Mitch rode out to the old family farm and spent two weeks cleaning up the place and hauling off rotten lumber and other items. The fences were all down and needed to be replaced. Many of the fence posts had broken off leaving stubs in the ground.

One afternoon Jodi rode up in a buckboard and yelled at Mitch, "What are you doing, I have brought something for you." Mitch turned his head and saw Jodi approaching him with something in her arms.

"Mitch, I want you to have this, I baked today and thought I might bring you some homemade bread."

"Well, that is might nice of you Jodi, but you didn't have to ride clear out here to give me some bread" Mitch said.

"I thought you might like something homemade since it's been such a long time," Jodi replied.

"Let's go inside and get out of the heat. Why don't you cut off a couple of slices of bread and I'll grab some marmalade and a cup of water." Mitch remarked. After visiting about little things Mitch got up and said," I had better get back to work and let you ride back to town before Trent gets home, he'll be wondering where you are, Mitch said."

Jodi got up and gave Mitch a kiss on the cheek than said;" Will you come over for supper on Sunday? I am goin to fry a rabbit along with fresh fried potatoes. I know this is your favorite meal; Trent told me so."

"That sound wonderful, of course I'll be there. What time is best?"

"Say around 3:00 O'clock." "Thanks again for the bread and I will see you and Trent on Sunday," Mitch replied. The following Sunday Mitch joined Trent and Jody supper.

"I want to thank you both for a good time and great food. I can't remember a better meal since I left home, "Mitch said.

"Here, I will walk you out," Jodivolunteered.

"That won't be necessary, I can find my way to my horse, I think! "Mitch replied.

Jodi followed Mitch to his horse then reached up and kissed him on the lips," You are welcome anytime she said.

Without a word Mitch mounted his horse and rode off. He didn't know what to do or say; he knew whatever the situation this could never happen again. Two weeks passed when one morning Jodi rode up to the old house and tied up her horse.

"What are you doing here," Mitch yelled!

"Oh I was just out for a ride. Trent won't be home until late, he is doing inventory at the store. Would you rather I leave Mitch"?

"I just don't think this is a good idea, you coming out here alone and all."

"Aren't you at least going to invite me in, or just leave me standing and begging to come inside? You know it is really warm and I could use a glass of cool water," Jodi asked?

"You can go inside and rest for a while then you better get back to town, "Mitch said in a firm voice. Jodi climbed down from her horse and strolled towards the front door of the house then walked inside.

"I have work to finish up before the sun sets, so make you're self at home before you leave," Mitch said.

"Aren't you even going to come in and visit for a while, "Jodi asked?

"No I'm not,this has gone far enough, and besides, you have no right to traipse around after another man when you are married to a great guy. I think it's time for you to leave," Mitch said as he turned and continued working on the fence. Jodi ran outside and mounted her horse then galloped off without saying another word. Mitch knew he was headed for trouble. The only thing he thought of doing was to stay away from Jodi and his Brother. It would be obvious, but he felt he had no choice. Two weeks passed and Trent asked Mitch to go fishing. Mitch agreed and they went to their favorite fishing hole, not far from the farm. They enjoyed catching up with the old times and the things they did while growing up.

Trent got up and said he thought it was time to head back to town. "By the way, How come we haven't seen much of you lately"?

"Oh, I guess I've just been caught up in trying to get the old place fixed up, that's all, "Mitch replied.

"Brother, don't be a stranger, Jodi thinks you are mad or something and I told her that was not the case. Please come by when you can and we'll break out some good stuff for old times," Trent said as he climbed in the saddle and headed back to town. Mitch looked up and waved good bye. Mitch knew he could not put himself in a position with Jodi being the only one present. The following week Mitch took the buckboard into town for supplies. He pulled up in front of the feed store and gave Trent a list of supplies he needed. While Mitch and Trent were loading the buckboard Jodi showed up.

"I thought I heard your voice Mitch, what brings you to town? It seems like we never see you anymore. It's hard to believe you are so busy you don't have time for your brother and Sister-in-law, "Jodi joked in a laughing way.

"I'm trying to finish the west side where all the fencing blew down. Winter's not far out and I want to get as much done before the first snow, that's all," Mitch replied. The wagon was loaded and Mitch climbed back on top and headed back to the farm.

Several weeks passed and Mitch decided to go to a small pond east of the old homestead where he and Trent would swim and spend time together as kids. Mitch had ridden up near the bank of the pond then stripped down then threw his clothes over the saddle. Mitch worked his way out into the deeper part of the water when he thought he heard someone yell! He turned to find Jodi climbing down from her horse approaching him while taking off her blouse.

"What do you want? You shouldn't be here and put your blouse back on; after all you are a married woman."

"Oh you know, what I want; It's you, Mitch. I wanted you from the first time I laid my eyes on you, after you stepped off that stage," Jodi said. Mitch turned his back to Jodi and asked her not to come into the water.

"If you don't let me come in I am going to tell Trent you took advantage of me after riding out to visit, "Jodi replied.

"I don't care what you want or what you say, you're nothing but a tramp and the sad part;you're married to my brother, "Mitch said.

"You know what you are? You're nothing but a pathetic crippled one armed man that can't see a good thing when he sees it. You will regret this day; I promise you "Jodi threatened

"You may be right, but at least I'm not chasing another man being already married.

Jodi buttoned up her blouse then turned away climbing back on her horse riding towards town. Mitch was sickened by what had happened; he knew Trent would never believe him if he told him the truth about Jodi, but he had to try. Mitch put his clothes on then rode back to town to try to explain to Trent what was going on. Mitch was about a mile out of town when he saw Trent riding towards him as fast as he could. Apparently Jodi had gotten to him first and told him a bunch of lies. Both Trent and Mitch abruptly stopped their horses.

Trent jumped down and said," Mitch, I'm going to kill you for what you've done to my wife."

"Please wait a minute, let me at least give you my side of the story," Mitch requested.

"There is nothing to discuss, I am going to draw on three, so you better be ready, "Trent insisted. About that time Jodi was riding toward them as fast as she could. Before she arrived Trent drew and shot his brother. Mitch fell to the ground, he had not reached for his gun; he would never draw on his brother. Trent ran to his brother lying on the ground with blood pouring out of his chest and mouth. Mitch tried to whisper something to Trent but it was too late he was dead.

Jodi jumped off her horse and screamed," Mitch can't be dead! This whole thing is my fault. I am the one that caused the problem, I made up the part about Mitch taking advantage of me by tearing off my blouse," Jodi yelled!

"You mean you made up the whole story about my brother? What kind of a woman would do such a terrible thing? You made me kill my brother! I thought Mitch was after you all along and all the while it was you," Trent said in a fit of rage, then turned his gun towards Jodi and shot her twice. She fell to the ground dead. Trent had lost his wife and only brother because of deceit and lies. Trent loaded the two bodies on each of their horse and took them to town. Trent told the sheriff what happened and turned him self in.

There was a trial with people arriving from everywhere to find out what happened. Trent was found not guilty in the killing of his brother but guilty of first degree murder in killing his wife in cold blood.

Trent was sentenced to hang for the death of Jodi. This was the first hanging in this small town in over twenty years.